The moving finger writes,
and having writ

Moves on; nor all your
piety nor wit

Shall lure it back to cancel
half a line

Nor all your tears wash
out a word of it.

Stanza 71
The Rubaiyat of
Omar Khayyam

LITHO BY WALSWORTH PUB. CO., INC., MARCELINE, MO.

# IN THE LAND OF CAVE
# AND CLIFF DWELLERS

BY

LIEUT. FREDERICK SCHWATKA, *1849–1892.*

AUTHOR OF "THE CHILDREN OF THE COLD," "NIMROD IN
THE NORTH; OR, HUNTING AND FISHING ADVEN-
TURES IN THE ARCTIC REGIONS," ETC.

*ILLUSTRATED*

The Rio Grande Press, Inc.

GLORIETA, NEW MEXICO · 87535

© 1977
The Rio Grande Press, Inc.,
Glorieta, N. M. 87535

First edition from which this edition
was reproduced was supplied by
William E. Sagstetter
Independent Filmmaker
P. O. Box 18579
Denver, Colo. 80218

NEW MATERIAL

1. New Publisher's Preface.
2. New scholarly Introduction by Bernard Fontana, Ph.D.
   (a) New bibliography by Dr. Fontana
   (b) New map of Schwatka's route based on
       information supplied by Dr. Fontana.
3. New index by Katherine McMahon, Albuquerque, N.M.
4. Eight new color photographs on endsheets, taken
   by Fr. Luis G. Verplancken, S.J.

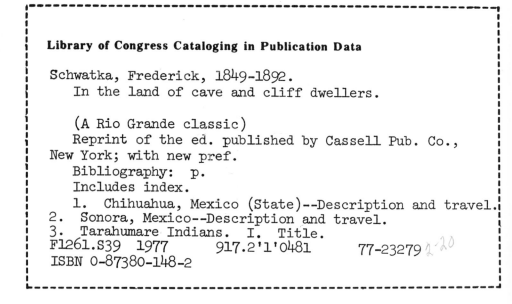

Library of Congress Cataloging in Publication Data

Schwatka, Frederick, 1849-1892.
   In the land of cave and cliff dwellers.

   (A Rio Grande classic)
   Reprint of the ed. published by Cassell Pub. Co.,
New York; with new pref.
   Bibliography:  p.
   Includes index.
   1.  Chihuahua, Mexico (State)--Description and travel.
2.  Sonora, Mexico--Description and travel.
3.  Tarahumare Indians.  I.  Title.
F1261.S39  1977      917.2'1'0481      77-23279 2-20
ISBN 0-87380-148-2

A RIO GRANDE CLASSIC
First published in 1893

First Printing 1977

The Rio Grande Press, Inc.

GLORIETA, NEW MEXICO · 87535

Next Two Pages

Map of Schwatka's Route, intended
only as a frame of reference.

Schwatka's Travels in Sonora and Chihuahua

# Publisher's Preface

We like to think we are familiar with the titles of books in the bibliography of the Southwest, which geographically and anthropologically must include some of Northwestern Mexico. We haven't, of course, read all of those thousands of books, but in studying bibliographies, one becomes accustomed to *titles*, if not contents. We have published several distinguished volumes dealing mainly with the Indians of Northwestern Mexico, the two most recent ones being *The Tarahumara; An Indian Tribe of Northern Mexico*, by Bennett and Zingg, and *Unknown Mexico*, by Carl Lumholtz. These two titles, plus a paperbound edition of *The Tarahumar of Mexico*, by Campbell Pennington (University of Utah Press, 1963) are the major publications in English on these reclusive remnants of American aborigines.

To make a short story long, we participated in the annual conference of the Western History Association in Denver last October, and during the book exhibit hours we had a visitor by the name of William E. Sagstetter. He had, he said, heard about our then newly-released *The Tarahumara* and he was anxious to obtain a copy. He is an "independent filmmaker" (on his own, as it were), and it seems he had recently gone to the Copper (Urique) Canyon country and made some motion picture footage for a television program on the Tarahumara Indians. He knew our

9

Bennett and Zingg title, and indeed, had used it, but the pictures he had obtained were not comparable to the color photographs we had in our book, pictures taken by Father Luis G. Verplancken, S.J., director of the Jesuit Tarahumara Mission at Creel in Chihuahua.

One thing of course led to another; we talked. He returned another day with a copy of a book we had never seen mentioned in the bibliographies — this one. We borrowed it, and were astounded to read in it an account of a white man's contact with the Tarahumara Indians that antedated that of Carl Lumholtz — long thought by most scholars to be the first.

In due course we passed this book along to our expert "in residence", so to speak, Dr. Bernard (Bunny) Fontana, of the staff at the Museum of Arizona (University of Arizona) in Tucson. He reported to us that he found it anthropologically worth reprinting, and not only that, it was — he said — a delightful book to read. With Mr. Sagstetter's approval and with Dr. Fontana's fine Introduction following our words, we present the 117th beautiful Rio Grande Classic. We greatly appreciate Mr. Sagstetter loaning us his rare first edition to reproduce ours, and we are indebted greatly to the scholarly knowledge and level-headed common sense of our friend Bunny Fontana.

Mr. Sagstetter's first edition was not in very good shape, however. Some pages were missing. The only other copy of the book in New Mexico appears to be a similar first edition in the library of the Laboratory of Anthropology of the Museum of New Mexico. Through the cooperation of librarian Margo Lamb, we were able to procure a copy of the missing pages. The book is not well known; our usual rare book sources drew a blank, and even some of the Mexican "specialists" in rare books didn't know this title. It does not appear in most bibliographies. The author is well enough known for his writings about the Arctic North, but this one small volume on the American Southwest (the Mexican Northwest) is all he ever did in this geographic area. Dr. Fontana lists Schwatka's other works in his (Fontana's) Introduction following.

The first edition of this rare title was printed (and atrociously so) by the late Cassell Publishing Company of New York in 1893. Schwatka speaks of his camera, and of taking photographs, but none of these appear in the book. What *is* there, as illustrations, is a series of ridiculous sketches drawn by who knows whom . . . the author, perhaps? We suspect the publisher located some talentless "artist" with no imagination at all who made the bad drawings from bad photographs; whatever the case, the illustrations are wretched. We would have left them out altogether, except that they are integrated into the layout of the signature as folio pages (but without folio numbers), so we couldn't. But the bad art work isn't all; the book was originally printed on sulphite paper, so that the pages after 83 years are brittle and discolored and very hard to handle. It might be said that we have "rescued" this book from oblivion in the very nick of time.

We have photographically enlarged the block of copy on each page, mainly to make the margins more proportionate to the text. The first edition was in dimensions four and one half inches by six inches, about the size of a modern "pocket" book. Our edition is the standard six inches by nine inches. Also, the first edition was not indexed. We called on our friend Katherine McMahon of Albuquerque (again, as we have often done before), who, though ailing, turned in quickly another of her excellent and professional indexes. We are most grateful for her willing cooperation under personal difficulties.

We might mention in passing that indexing this book may have been largely an exercise in futility. Many of Schwatka's villages and stopping places are not on any map and indeed, may not even exist any more. More than that, who these days would ever attempt to follow Schwatka's romantic journey? The first edition had no map, either, probably because the area covered was so large and so remote no one could make a map of it. By guesswork, by a large topographical Mexican map and by following the text of the book, Dr. Fontana reconstructed the route *approximately.* We went ahead and made a frame of reference map which merely *suggests* Schwatka's route. By and large, the author made a simple circle tour through the roughest country in Mexico and perhaps in the Northern hemisphere, ending up eventually where he began in Mexico, at Cd. Chihuahua.

Schwatka's interest in the Tarahumara Indians that he encountered throughout his journey was not the interest of a scientist, or even a scholar, and indeed, one finishes reading the book without any real perception of these strange people. Schwatka was writing a travel book, and the reader gets the impression that everything else was subordinate to that goal. After his many experiences with the Arctic Indians and the Indians of the American Southwest, the Tarahumara Indians may not have been the "novelty" to him they might have been to one less blasé about aborigines. But his account of an eventful, dangerous and fascinating hike in the Mexican wilderness is bright and breezy and interesting to read. The armchair traveler will find it engrossing from beginning to end, merely as a story of high and low adventure.

We should account ourselves for the eight color photographs appearing on the endpapers. These were selected from the 385 new color pictures we added to our edition of *The Tarahumara; An Indian Tribe of Northern Mexico;* they were taken by Father Luis G. Verplancken, S.J., the director of the Jesuit Mission to the Indians at Creel, on the edge of Copper (Urique) Canyon country. The full story of how we came to publish the Bennett and Zingg title and how we obtained the use of the extraordinary photographs of Father Verplancken, is set forth in our edition. It was difficult to select just eight photographs out of 385, but these − far better than the unfortunate sketches in the book − offer a quick look at the land and the people Frederick Schwatka writes about. For those more interested in anthropology and ethnology then in travel, we suggest you buy or borrow from your local library a copy of our Bennett and Zingg reprint.

While this is not in itself a book for the researcher and historian, it *is* source material and it *is* an interesting and valuable supplement to other titles on the Indians of the American Southwest and the Mexican Northwest. And if your bag happens to be backpacking in a wilderness, you would do well to take this book along if you go hiking in Tarahumaraland.

Robert B. McCoy

La Casa Escuela
Glorieta, New Mexico 87535
December 1976

# Introduction

In the year of the Lord 1607 Father Juan Fonte, a member of the
Society of Jesus and a native of Barcelona, Spain, came face to face
with natives of the mountains and canyons of southwestern
Chihuahua. These were the Rarámuri or "foot runners" as they
called themselves, a term which fell on Spanish ears as
"Tarahumar." They were locked in warfare along their southeast-
ern border with neighboring Tepehuanes, perhaps an agitation
resulting from the latters' moving northward away from Spanish
presence to their south. In any event, it was Father Fonte's hope
that a peace could be effected between these opposing groups of
Indians, and in 1607, with a trusted Tepehuán leader at his side, he
held a friendly conference with 842 Tarahumar men (Dunne 1948:
14-15; Pennington 1963: 1, 14).

Within a few years of Father Fonte's initial *entrada* the Jesuits
began to plant missions in Tarahumar country. Spanish ranches
and farms and cities grew near their boundaries. Mining centers
were established within their territory at Coyáchi (1684),
Cusihuiriachic (1687), Urique (1691), Loreto (1707), Batopilas
(1708), Uriachic (1736), and Chínipas (1758). By 1693 Don Joseph
Francisco Marın was able to report that Tarahumares living in the
eastern and northern portions of their country were busy farming,
raising livestock, and were behaving generally much as did

Spaniards of the same region (Pennington 1963: 18-23).

This is not to suggest that the hispanicization of Tarahumares proceeded smoothly and apace among all of them. There were major Indian rebellions in parts of Tarahumar country in 1630, 1652, and 1690. By the early 18th century, however, Jesuit missions were firmly established or re-established throughout most of the region, and as early as 1753 some of the Tarahumares were deemed to have become sufficiently Christianized and hispanicized that a few of the missions were advanced from Jesuit control to that of the secular clergy. In the view of the Spanish Crown, this was the ultimate step on the road to complete assimilation of the native population (Pennington 1963: 15-16).

The Jesuits were expelled from all of New Spain in 1767, and they were replaced in the Tarahumar posts by friars of the Franciscan Order. A shortage of priestly personnel and disagreements concerning whether the churches should be missions (and thereby tax exempt) or curacies under secular clergy led to a general disintegration of the missions, a situation which persisted until the return of Jesuits to modern Mexico and specifically to Tarahumar country in 1900 (Pennington 1963: 16).

All the while Spanish and, subsequently, Mexican mining activities continued. The silver workings which had been started near the Batopililla Indians — a group of Tarahumares — in the early 18th century grew eventually to become Batopilas, Chihuahua, and the base of operations of the Batopilas Mining Company of New York, a firm started with an authorized capital of $9,000,000. The company was incorporated October 13, 1887. It consolidated older companies and bought others outright (Pletcher 1958: 193-194).

It appears that trends begun among Tarahumares at least as early as the beginnings of the 17th century persisted for 350 years if not, indeed, until today. This consisted of some of these people becoming mestizoized or otherwise surrendering their native identities; some of them maintaining their identities but accomodating in large measure to the presence of non-Indians and becoming an integral part of the non-Indian economy of the region; and some of them withdrawing into isolation, retreating from the outside world to subsist on whatever natural and economic resources might be at hand, including Spanish-introduced livestock.

Such was the setting in 1890 when Frederick Schwatka, M.D., arctic explorer, and former 1st lieutenant, United States Army, came riding onto the stage via muleback. He was, as he writes in the preface to this book, under contract to the Chicago *Herald* to visit the mountain fastness of southwestern Chihuahua and to describe its Indians and its mines for readers of newspapers.

Frederick Schwatka was born September 29, 1849, in Galena, Illinois. His father was Frederick Schwatka, a cooper by trade. His family took him to Salem, Oregon, when he was ten years old. He went to school, worked as a printer, and spent a short time at Wilamette University. In 1867 he was given an appointment to the United States Military Academy at West Point. He graduated with a commission as 2nd lieutenant in the 2nd cavalry on June 12, 1871. From October 20, 1871, to November 28 of the same year he was involved in conducting troops to Arizona. Subsequent assignments took him to various military posts in Nebraska where he remained until September 24, 1875, having spent from August 13 through October of 1872 on the Big Horn expedition (New York *Times* 1892).

Between September 25, 1875, and March 14, 1876, Schwatka took the first of five military leaves of absence. From April 9 to May 18, 1876, he was assigned to Fort D.A. Russell in Wyoming, and from May 9 through October 24, 1876, he was on the Big Horn and Yellowstone expedition. His next stations were at Camp Sheridan, Nebraska, and the Spotted Tail Agency in Dakota Territory. From October 1, 1880 to May 14, 1881, he was on special duty in New York City from which he was sent back to Fort D.A. Russell, Wyoming where he became ill, took sick leave and another leave of absence (New York *Times* 1892).

Schwatka was aide de camp to Brigadier General Nelson Miles from October 21, 1881, to May 8, 1884, this service being punctuated by a leave of absence and an exploring trip to Alaska. His final real military assignment was at Fort Thomas, Arizona, where he served from May of 1884 until August 2 of that year. He was called to Portland, Oregon, to testify as a witness before the United States court there, and from September 6, 1884 to January 31, 1885, he was on leave of absence. He resigned from the army at the end of his leave, January 31, 1885 (New York *Times* 1892).

During his military career Schwatka had been promoted to 1st lieutenant in the 1st cavalry March 20, 1879, and he had availed himself of various opportunities to study both law and medicine. He was admitted to the Nebraska bar in 1875; in 1876 he received a medical degree from Bellevue Hospital Medical College in New York City (Johnson and Malone 1937: 481). But it was neither as soldier nor lawyer nor doctor that Schwatka came best to be known to a late 19th-century public. It was instead as explorer and writer. As explained in the *Dictionary of American Biography* (Johnson and Malone 1937: 481):

. . . He became interested in exploration, and his adventurous imagination was seized by reports brought from the Arctic regions by Capt. Thomas F. Barry concerning the fate of the famous expedition of Sir John Franklin [in 1947]. For thirty years following the loss of this expedition British and American explorers had sought the bodies or the papers of the Franklin party. Schwatka persuaded the American Geographical Society to organize a new search in the Arctic. [He obtained a leave of absence from the Army.] This expedition, commanded by Schwatka and William Henry Golder of the *New York Herald,* sailed from New York on June 19, 1878, in the *Eothen.* The explorers did not return for more than two years. During their search in King William Land in 1879-1880 they performed the longest sledge journey then on record, being absent from their base of supplies for eleven months and twenty days and traversing 2,819 geographical or 3,251 statute miles. Schwatka's search resolved the last doubts about the fate of the Franklin expedition. He discovered the wreckage of one untraced ship, located many of the graves of members of the party, gave other mortal remains decent burial, brought back various relics, and established beyond doubt that Franklin's records were lost. "Schwatka's search," described by Gilder in articles in the *Herald,* became a popular phrase, and his discoveries were hailed as a triumph of Arctic exploration.

In 1886, this time under the patronage of the New York *Times,* Schwatka returned to the Arctic for further explorations. These various efforts brought him the Roquette Arctic medal from the Geographical Society of Paris, a medal from the Imperial Geographical Society of Russia, and honorary memberships in the geographical societies of Berlin, Geneva, and Roma (National Cyclopaedia of American Biography 1893; Wilson and Fiske 1888).

In 1889 and 1890 Schwatka made three forays into northwestern Mexico, the subjects of this book. The first was from Deming, New Mexico, south to the prehistoric ruins of Casas Grandes, Chihuahua, which Schwatka colorfully labelled a "Toltec Babylon." Since 1889 these magnificent ruins have been excavated and studied in minute detail by archaeologist Charles C. DiPeso (1974), whose eight-volume report is a labor worthy of the ruins themselves. Just as Casas Grandes is today a Mexican National Monument, so are DiPeso's efforts to understand the secrets locked within her material remains a landmark in the history of archaeological publication for the Southwest.

Enroute to Casas Grandes Schwatka passed through the Mormon settlement of Colonia Díaz, one of four such communities then in Chihuahua. Somewhat prophetically, he noted (p. 40): ". . . they [Mormons] never will predominate politically or in numbers over the other inhabitants if we include the Mexican population, which is almost universally Catholic." It turned out to be worse than that. Between 1885 and 1909 the Mormons founded nine *colonias* in northern Mexico, six in Chiahuahua and three in eastern Sonora. The dictator Porfirio Díaz, who had given the Mormons permission to settle in Mexico, fell from power in May, 1911. By the end of the summer of 1912 most Mormons had been forced to flee from Mexico; by the end of 1914 all of them had left the country (Burns and Naylor 1973: 143-144, 173-176).

Schwatka also speaks on 1889 speculation concerning the possibility of a railroad through western Chiahuahua. The possibility became a reality, and today a main line runs from El Paso, Texas, and Ciudad Juarez, Chiahuahua, southward along the eastern edge of the Sierra Madre, with a connecting northeast-southwest link which runs across the Sierra Madre through Creel and down to the west coast of Sonora and the Gulf of California.

Schwatka's second Mexican sojourn was by train from Deming, New Mexico, to the Sonoran west coast at the port city of Guaymas. To make the journey he rode via Southern Pacific from Deming to Benson, Arizona, and then from Benson to Nogales, Sonora, on "The Burro," the New Mexico and Arizona Railroad which was completed in 1882 to link up with the Sonora Railway from Guaymas (Myrick 1975: 263-302), His trip to the Mexican west coast was characterized chiefly by a javelina hunt, although his description of Guaymas is interesting if only because it tells us something about this place — which has since become a favorite vacation spot for beach-loving North Americans — in the late 19th century.

The third and final foray into Mexico was the longest and the most unusual (see chapters IV-X). In making this expedition and writing about it Schwatka became the first American observor to visit Tarahumar Indians and to publish an extended description of them in English. Five years earlier, the physician-botanist-naturalist Edward Palmer had spent from August through December, 1885, in Tarahumar country collecting botanical specimens for the Smithsonian Institution, but only his botanical notes seem to have survived if, indeed, he made any others. In any case, he never published a word concerning the Tarahumar (see Watson 1886 for a list of the plants collected by Palmer; also see Beaty 1964: 161-165 and McVaugh 1956: 90-92 for brief discussions of his 1885 Chihuahuan expedition).

Palmer and Schwatka were both in the Southwest in the early 1870s. Although no evidence has come to light thus far to indicate that they knew one another, there remains at least the possibility that Schwatka may have been drawn to northwestern Mexico and Tarahumar country through having heard about them from Palmer; it is also possible that Schwatka's newspaper articles and lectures may have drawn the attention of Carl Lumholtz to the region. If this is so, however, Lumholtz makes no mention of it (Lumholtz 1973: vii-xix). And the present volume was published originally after Lumholtz had already been among the Tarahumares.

In any event, Schwatka's name has to rank high on the list of 19th century English-speaking observors of southwestern Chihuahua. His tracks were later to be followed by Lumholtz (1973), Bennett and Zingg (1976), Pennington (1963) and others, all of whom have greatly expanded our knowledge of Tarahumar and of the region in which they continue to reside. There are published works earlier than this one of Schwatka based on first hand observations, but these are in languages other than English. The two most notable are those of Steffel (1809) and Tellechea (1826), the latter a priest writing a Tarahuma grammar to make it possible for his fellow clergymen to administer the sacraments of the Catholic Church in the native language (see Murdock and O'Leary 1975: V: 353-358 for a 155-entry bibliography of Tarahumar studies).

During his circuit of Tarahumar country, from Cusihuiriachic to Cusihuiriachic, Schwatka traversed some of the most rugged country in North America (see Heald 1958 for a good discussion of the terrain). He saw Tarahumar Indians in large numbers, dividing them into what he called "civilized" and "savage" population segments. The former were those who had integrated themselves into the non-Indian economy of the region and who either worked in mines or who lived permanently in large towns in the Mexican manner. The "savages" were no doubt those natives who chose to maintain their own lives and economy in their own fashion, and who withdrew as much as possible from dealings with the outside world in an effort to maintain some semblance of cultural autonomy.

Although the terrain is rugged, with high mountain plateaus interlaced with deep canyons and steep trails, it was well-traveled even in 1890. If Tarahumares were not running up and down precipitous paths, then mules and burros were, carrying passengers, silver ore, mining equipment, supplies, and luxuries to the incredibly rich mines at Urique and Batopilas. Schwatka says that the mines at Urique date from 1612; later research shows the date to be 1691. Similarly, he dates the mines at Batopilas from 1632 when the accurate date is 1708 (Pennington 1963: 21). Regardless of their dates of discovery, in 1890 they were doing very well. Schwatka speaks of the "castle-like" structure that was the hacienda of part owner and mine superintendent Alexander R. Shepherd at Batopilas. He notes the "great conglomeration of buildings . . . lighted by electricity and furnished with all modern conveniences, including hot and cold water, steam baths, and, an unusual luxury, an immense swimming pool, formed by a slight deflection of a portion of the Batopilas River" (pp. 312-313). Before Shepherd's death in 1902, he even imported an upright piano. The Tarahumares lashed the piano to heavy poles on either side and working in three relays of eight men, relieving each other every twenty minutes, they carted the heavy instrument 185 miles over the mountains (Pletcher 1958: 201). Shepherd, an engineer who had been Washington, D.C.'s vice-chairman (and not the governor, as Schwatka says) and director of public works, was not to deny himself and his family what he apparently considered to be the rudiments of civilization (good discussions of Shepherd and the Batopilas mines are in Pletcher 1958: 182-218 and Shepherd 1938).

Another entrepreneur in northern Mexico to whom Schwatka alludes, although not by name, was Albert K. Owen (see pages 336-338). This concerned Owen's utopian colony at Topolobampo on the west coast of Sonora and his dreams of a railroad to link the colony with Texas (see Moore 1975; Robertson 1947; Pletcher 1958: 106-148). He died several decades before the *Ferrocarril de Chiahuahua al Pacifico* belatedly turned his dream into reality.

When Schwatka left Mexico after his Tarahumar trip he had little time left to live. A policeman found him at 3:00 a.m. on Wednesday, November 2, 1892, lying in the streets of Portland, Oregon. He had been out to dinner with a friend the evening before. At first the policeman thought he was drunk, but it soon became obvious he was not. At 4:00 a.m. that same morning, Lieutenant Frederick Schwatka, Arctic explorer and Mexican adventurer, died in Good Samaritan Hospital from what turned out to be an accidental overdose of laudanum, an opium derivative. As explained in the front page obituary of the New York *Times* (1892): "His life had been marked by such a degree of convivialities that his stomach had of recent years given him much trouble, and for the purpose of finding relief he used small quantities of laudanum . . ." A half-filled bottle was found next to him on the Portland street.

According to a friend, at the time of his death Schwatka was making plans to return soon to Mexico, "where he had a gigantic scheme with some Mexican land company." His newspaper obituaries refer to two sisters living in Salem, Oregon, and to an uncle living in Ukiah, California, but make no mention of his wife (New York *Times* 1892). That he once had a wife, however, seems apparent in that a book by A. C. Harris (1897) contains a section called, "Mrs. Schwatka's recollections of her husband as the Alaska pathfinder."

With this re-publication of *In the Land of Cave and Cliff Dwellers* by the Rio Grande Press, perhaps Schwatka will now be remembered for more than his Alaska adventures alone. He can now claim his rightful place in the history of travel and description of northern Mexico, and most particularly of southwestern Chiahuahua.

Bernard L. Fontana

Arizona State Museum
The University of Arizona, Tucson
November, 1976

# Bibliography

Beaty, Janice J.
1964          *Plants in his pack.* New York, Pantheon Books.


Bennett, Wendell C., and Robert M. Zingg
1967          *The Tarahumara. An Indian tribe of northern
              Mexico.* Glorieta, New Mexico, The Rio Grande
              Press, Inc. [Republication of the 1935 edition,
              with added materials and 385 new color
              photographs.]


Burns, Barney T., and Thomas H. Naylor
1973          Colonia Morelos: a short history of a Mormon
              colony in Sonora, Mexico. *The Smoke Signal*, no.
              27 (Spring), pp. 141-180. Tucson, Tucson Corral
              of the Westerners.


DiPeso, Charles C.
1974          *Casas Grandes. A fallen trading center of the
              Gran Chichimeca.* Eight volumes. Flagstaff,
              Arizona, Northland Press.


Dunne, Peter M.
1948          *Early Jesuit missions in Tarahumara.* Berkeley
              and Los Angeles, University of California Press.


Harris, A. C.
1897          *Alaska and the Klondike gold fields.* Philadel-
              phia, National Publishing Company.


Heald, Weldon F.
1958          How deep are those Mexican barrancas? *Pacific
              Discovery*, Vol. 11, no. 4 (September-October),
              pp. 22-27. San Francisco, California Academy of
              Sciences.

Johnson, Allen, ad Dumas Malone, *editors*
1937          Schwatka, Frederick. *Dictionary of American Biography*, Vol. 16, pp. 481-482. New York, Charles Scribner's Sons.


Lumholtz, Carl
1973          *Unknown Mexico*. Two volumes. Glorieta, New Mexico, The Rio Grande Press, Inc. [Re-publication, with new materials and new color photographs, of the 1902 edition.]


McVaugh, Rogers
1956          *Edward Palmer*. Norman, University of Oklahoma Press.


Moore, Charles W.
1975          Paradise at Topolobampo. *The Journal of Arizona History*, Vol. 16, no. 1 (Spring), pp. 1-28. Tucson, Arizona Historical Society.


Murdock, George P., and Timothy J. O'Leary
1975          *Ethnographic bibliography of North America*. Five volumes. New Haven, Connecticut, Human Relations Area Files Press.


Myrick, David F.
1975          *Railroads of Arizona*. Volume 1. Berkeley, California, Howell-North Books.


The National Cyclopaedia of American Biography
1893          Schwatka, Frederick. *The National Cyclopaedia of American Biography*. Vol. 3, p. 285. New York, James T. White & Co.

New York *Times*
1892            Lieut. Frederick Schwatka is dead. *The New York Times* (newspaper), Thursday, November 3 (Vol. 42, no. 12,853), p. 1, col. 3. New York City.


Pennington, Campbell W.
1963            *The Tarahumar of Mexico.* Salt Lake City, University of Utah Press.


Pletcher, David M.
1958            *Rails, mines, and progress. Seven American promoters in Mexico, 1867-1911.* Ithaca, New York, Cornell University Press.


Robertson, Thomas A.
1947            *Southwestern utopia.* Los Angeles, Ward Ritchie Press.


Schwatka, Frederick
1880            Arctic meeting at Chickering hall, October 28th, 1880. Reception of Lieut. Frederick Schwatka and his associates of the Franklin search party of 1878, 1879 and 1880. Addresses by Chief-Justice Daly, Lieut. Frederick Schwatka, U. S. Army, and Dr. Isaac I. Hayes. *Journal of the American Geographical Society*, Vol. 12, pp. 237-296. New York.


1883            The igloo of the Innuit. *Science*, Vol. 2, no. 28 (August 17), pp. 182-186; no. 29 (August 24), pp. 216-218; no. 30 (August 31), pp. 259-262; no. 31 (September 7), pp. 304-306; no. 32 (September 14), pp. 347-349. Cambridge, Massachusetts, The Science Company.

1884a    The Alaska military reconnaissance of 1883. *Science*, Vol. 3, no. 55 (February 22), pp. 220-227; no. 56 (February 29), pp. 246-252. Cambridge, Massachusetts, The Science Company.

1884b    An arctic vessel and her equipment. *Science*, Vol. 3, no. 64 (April 25), pp. 505-511. Cambridge, Massachusetts, The Science Company.

1884c    Exploration of the Yukon river in 1883. *Journal of the American Geographical Society*. Vol. 16, pp. 345-382. New York.

1884d    Icebergs and ice-floes. *Science*, Vol. 3, no. 65 (May 2), pp. 535-538. Cambridge, Massachusetts, The Science Company.

1884e    The middle Yukon. *Science*, Vol. 3, no. 70 (June 6), pp. 677-682; no. 71 (June 13), pp. 706-711. Cambridge, Massachusetts, The Science Company.

1884f    The Netschilluk Innuits. *Science*, Vol. 4, no. 98 (December 19), pp. 543-545. Cambridge, Massachusetts, The Science Company.

1884g    Wintering in the arctic. *Science*, Vol. 3, no. 66 (May 9), pp. 566-571. Cambridge, Massachusetts, The Science Company.

[1885]a   *Along Alaska's great rivers. A popular account of the travels of the Alaska exploring expedition of 1883, along the great Yukon river, from its source to its mouth, in the British. North-west territory, and in the territory of Alaska.* New York, Cassell and Company, Limited.

1885b      *Nimrod in the north; or, Hunting and fishing adventures in the arctic regions.* New York, Cassell and Company, Ltd.

1885c      The north magnetic pole. *Science*, Vol. 5, no. 108 (February 27), pp. 164-165. Cambridge, Massachusetts, The Science Company.

1885d      Report of a military reconnaissance in Alaska, made in 1883, by Frederick Schwatka. *Senate Executive Documents*, no. 2, 48th Congress, 2nd session. Washington, D.C., Government Printing Office.

1886a      Ascent of Mount St. Elias: Alaska territory. *Scottish Geographical Magazine*, Vol. 2, no. 10 (October), pp. 689-693. Edinburgh, Scottish Geographical Society.

1886b      *The children of the cold.* New York, Cassell and Company, Ltd.

1886c      Eskimo building-snow. *Science*, Vol. 7, no. 154 (January 15), pp. 54-55. New York, The Science Company.

1887      Among the Apaches. *The Century*, Vol. 34 (new series Vol. 12), no. 1 (May), pp. 41-52. New York, The Century Company; London, T. Fisher Unwin.

1890a      The pre-historic men with Lieutenant Frederick Schwatka. *The Naturalist*, Vol. 4, no. 7 (February), Kansas City, Missouri, Kansas City Academy of Sciences.

1890b      The sun-dance of the Sioux. *The Century*, Vol. 39 (new series Vol. 17), no. 5 (March), pp. 753-759. New York, The Century Company; London, T. Fisher Unwin.

1891      *A summer in Alaska. A popular account of the travels of an Alaska exploring expedition along the great Yukon river, from its source to its mouth, in the British Northwest territory, and in the territory of Alaska.* Philadelphia, J. Y. Huber Company. [An enlarged edition of Schwatka 1885a.]

1892      *Nimrod in the north, or Hunting and fishing adventures in the arctic regions.* New York, Cassell Publishing Company.

1893a      *In the land of cave and cliff dwellers.* New York, Cassell Publishing Company.

1893b      *A summer in Alaska.* St. Louis, Missouri, J. W. Henry. [A reprint of Schwatka 1891.]

1899a      *The children of the cold.* New York, Chicago [etc.], Education Publishing Company. [A reprint of Schwatka 1886b.]

1899b      *In the land of cave and cliff dwellers.* Boston, New York [etc.], Educational Publishing Company. [A reprint of Schwatka 1893a.]

1902      *The children of the cold.* Boston, New York [etc.], Educational Publishing Company. [A reprint of Schwatka 1886b.]

1930        *The children of the cold.* Springfield, Massachusetts, The H. R. Huntting Co., Inc. [A reprint of Schwatka 1886b.]

1974        *Among the Apaches.* Palmer Lake, Colorado, The Filter Press. [A reprint of Schwatka 1887.]

Schwatka, Frederick; Rose G. Kingsley, B. P. Shillaber, and other
1886        *Stories of danger and adventure.* Boston, D. Lothrop and Company.

Shepherd, Grant
1938        *The silver magnet.* New York, E.P. Dutton and Company.

Steffel, Matthäus
1809        Tarahumarisches wortebuch, nebst einigen nachrichten von den sitten und gebrauchen der Tarahumaren, in Neu Biscaya, in der audiencia Guadalaxara im vice-konigreiche Alt-Mexico, oder New-Spanien. In *Nachrichten von verschiedenen ländern des spanischen Amerika,* edited by Christoph G. von Murr, Vol. 1, no. 11, pp. 293-374. Halle.

Tellechea, Miguel
1826        *Compendio gramatical para le inteligencia del idioma tarahumar.* México, Impr. de la Federación en palacio.

Watson, Sereno
1886        List of plants collected by Dr. Edward Palmer in south-western Chihuahua, Mexico in 1885. *Proceedings of the American Academy of Arts and Sciences,* Vol. 21, pp. 414-455. Boston, John Wilson and son.

Wilson, James G., and John Fiske, *editors*
1888        Schwatka, Frederick. *Appleton's Cyclopaedia of American Biography,* Vol. 5, p. 433. New York, D. Appleton and Company.

# IN THE LAND OF CAVE
## AND CLIFF DWELLERS

BY

LIEUT. FREDERICK SCHWATKA

AUTHOR OF "THE CHILDREN OF THE COLD," "NIMROD IN
THE NORTH; OR, HUNTING AND FISHING ADVEN-
TURES IN THE ARCTIC REGIONS," ETC.

---

*ILLUSTRATED*

---

NEW YORK
## THE CASSELL PUBLISHING CO.
104 AND 106 FOURTH AVENUE

THE MERSHON COMPANY PRESS,
RAHWAY, N.° J.

# PREFACE.

————

THIS book records in a popular way the adventures, researches, and other doings of two expeditions sent into Northern Mexico in the years 1889 and 1890, the patron of the first being *America* and of the other *The Herald*, both Chicago publications. The story is told, however, as if it were a continuous undertaking, to make it more succinct and interesting; the public probably being uninterested in the business details, which did not vary from the usual details of that nature.

In this light the Mexican expedition

easily divides itself into three quite
distinct trips, the first from Deming,
N. M., southward into the northwestern
part of the State of Chihuahua; the
second through the central part of the
State of Sonora; and the third and most
important from the city of Chihuahua,
in the State of the same name, westward
into the Sierra Madre range, that forms
the boundary between the States of
Sonora and Chihuahua on the northern
part of the travels, and Durango and
Sinaloa on the southern.

None of the travels can be strictly
called exploration, although often alluded
to as such in the American press, yet
there were a few interesting and impor-
ant facts disclosed by the researches that
almost amounted to discoveries in the
light of the very little that was generally

known regarding them. This was especially true of the living cliff and cave
dwellers found abiding in the Northern
Mexican Sierra Madres, the knowledge
of whose existence was seemingly con-
fined to the native *peons* and laborers but
little above them in the scale of intelli-
gence, on the one side, and an exceedingly few intelligent Mexicans and foreigners, mostly engaged in mining, on
the other, who either did not care to give
the world any accounts of these strange
beings or who had interests in keeping
everything regarding this rich country as
secret as possible. Quite a long residence, off and on, in our own Southwest
country had somewhat familiarized me
with the dwellings and relics of the cliff
and cave dwellers of that region, and, in
common with the general opinion, I

believed they belonged to a race wholly extinct, and with no direct or indirect living representatives, at least on the North American continent. Even when the first living cliff dwellers were found in Mexico I believed they were isolated cases of depraved savages having acquired ancient dwellings, as the very lowest order of our own people occasionally seek similar habitations on the outskirts of towns and cities. But I was certainly not prepared to believe that this singular and savage race was so extensively distributed and so distinct from all others in its characteristics; and this belief was undoubtedly universal, as shown in the comments elicited by the discovery. Whether there are any relations existing between the extinct cliff and cave dwellers of our own country and those now existing in Mexico is a technically scientific question that I was not prepared to investigate, both because the discovery was wholly unexpected, and (still more important) because destitute of a sufficient knowledge of the subject to do so. Had I been able to overcome both obstacles, however, I could have done no more than to leave the subject in the shape of an incomplete theory at the best, as all similar ethnological discussions have been left ; and I doubt if this would have added to or subtracted from the more definite purpose of being the first to consider them in any light whatsoever. Such information as I obtained regarding this most curious people and their strange country is related in the following pages.

FREDERICK SCHWATKA.

# CONTENTS.

IN THE LAND OF

# CAVE AND CLIFF DWELLERS.

---

## CHAPTER I.

NORTHWESTERN CHIHUAHUA — PREPARING
FOR THE EXPEDITION—FROM DEMING,
N. M., TO CASAS GRANDES, CHIHUAHUA.

THE first chapter describing an expedition is liable to be prosaic to the
point of dullness. It is full of promises
that are expected to be realized, while as
yet nothing has been done. Not one-
tenth of these may formulate, and yet the
expedition may be a success in unexpected results ; for in no undertaking is
there so much uncertainty as in travel

through little known countries.    Then,
again, the writer is likely to consider himself called upon to give a lengthy description of the party in the preliminary letter,
and, as I have often seen, even descend
to an enumeration of the qualities of the
cook or the color of the mules.    The
next night the cook may desert and the
mules may run away, so that others must
be procured, and therefore they are of no
more interest to the reader than any other
of the millions of cooks or mules that
would make any writer wealthy if he
could find a publisher who would print
his description of them.    I intend to
break away from that stereotyped for-
mula in this first chapter and briefly state
that I was in the field of Northern Mexico, hoping to obtain new and interesting
matter beyond the everlasting descrip-

tions that are now pumped up for the public by versatile writers along the beaten lines of tourist travel, as determined by the railroads, and, occasionally, the diligence lines. I had a good outfit of wagons, horses, mules, and last, but not least, men for that purpose. Each and every member of the expedition will be heard from when anything has been done by them, and not before. When the mule Dulce kicks a hectare of daylight through the cook for spilling hot grease on his heels I will give a description of Dulce and an obituary notice of the cook; but until then they will remain out of the account.

We crossed the boundary south of Deming early in March, 1889, and entered Mexican territory, where our travels can be said to have begun. If one

will take the pains to look at a map of
this portion of Mexico he will see that it
projects into the United States some distance beyond the average northern boundary, the Rio Grande being to our east,
and an " offset," as we would say in surveying, being to our west, this "offset"
running north and south.   This flat peninsula projecting into our own country
can be better understood by visiting it
and comparing it with the surrounding
land of the United States, coupled with a
history of the country.   Roughly speaking, the Mexican-United States boundary,
as settled by the Mexican War, followed
the line of the Southern Pacific Railway
as now constructed, and the so-called
Gadsden purchase from Mexico of a few
years later fixed the boundary as we now
see it, giving us a narrow, sabulous strip

OUTFITTING AT DEMING

of Mexican territory, but a definite boundary, easily established by surveys.

The Mexicans were on the ground and
knew just what they were doing when
they arranged for selling us this narrow
strip; while, as usual, we did everything
from Washington, and knew just about
as little concerning it as we possibly
could and be sure we were purchasing a
part of Mexico. The Mexicans ran this
flat-topped peninsula far to the north,
inclosing lakes, rivers, and springs, and
waters innumerable; while, as a generous compensation, they gave us more
land to the west, but a land where a
coyote carries three days' rations of
jerked jack rabbit whenever he makes up
his mind to cross it. There is no more
comparison between the offset of Mexico
that projects here into the United States,

and the offset from the United States
that projects into Mexico west of here,
than there is in comparing the fertile
plains of Iowa or Illinois with Greenland
or the Great Sahara Desert.

Everyone familiar with the exceedingly rich lands of the Southwest, when
so much of it is worthless for want of
water, knows how valuable that liquid is
in this region, especially if it occurs in
quantities sufficiently large for the purposes of irrigation.   I have stood on
land that I could purchase for five
cents an acre or less, and that stretched
out behind me for limitless leagues, and
could jump on other land whose owner
had refused a number of hundreds of
dollars an acre, although, as far as the
eye could see, there was no more difference between them than between any

two adjoining acres on an Illinois farm.
The real difference was one to be determined by the surveyor's level, which
showed that water could be put on the
valuable tract and not on the other.
This also is the difference between the
Mexican "offset" in the North, lying
between the Rio Grande and the me-
ridianal boundary to the west, and the
American tract that juts into Mexico just
west of this again. They both share the
same soil as you gaze at them from the
deck of your "burro," and you can even
see no difference in them on closer inspection, after your mule has assisted
you to alight; but there is a real and
tangible value difference of from one
hundred to two hundred dollars a year
per acre between the grapes and other
fruits and vegetables you can raise on

one, with water trickling round their roots, and the sagebrush and grease wood of the other, not rating at ten cents a township.

The diplomats of our country at Washington may be all Talleyrands in astuteness, but in the Gadsden purchase they got left so far behind that they have never yet been able to see how badly they were handled in the bargain.

As our people travel along the line of the Southern Pacific Railway, through its arid wastes of sand and sunshine, they can little realize the beautiful country of Northern Chihuahua and Sonora that lies so close to them to the southward. And yet some of this seemingly arid land in Southern New Mexico and Arizona is destined to become of far more value than its present appearance would indicate. Anglo-Saxon energy is converting little patches here and there into fertile spots, and these are constantly increasing. A great portion of the land is fine for cattle grazing, and these little oases make centers of crystallizing civilization, which render the country for miles around valuable for this important industry.

The persons who believe that New Mexico will not eventually become one of the finest States in our Union belong to the class of those who put Dakota, Nebraska, and Kansas in the great American desert a decade or two ago.

There is still another physical feature of at least Northern Mexico that I have never seen dwelt upon, even in the numerous physical geographies that are now extant, and it is well worth explaining.

Books innumerable have spoken of the *tierra caliente,* or low, hot lands near the coast, the *tierra templada,* or temperate lands of the interior plateaus, and the *tierra fria,* or cold lands of the mountains and higher plateaus ; and these subdivisions are really good as explaining Mexican climate, but they give us but little idea of the country's surface itself beyond that of altitude, and even less regarding its resources and adaptability to the wants of man. The *tierra caliente,* or hot lands of the coast, are out of the question as habitations for white men ; but the *tierra templada* and *tierra fria,* as everyone familiar with climatology knows, gives us the finest climate in the world, as do all elevated plateaus in sub. tropical countries. But these elevated plateaus, or different portions of them,

are not alike in resources, and their variations are simply due to the variations in
the water supply.

The backbone ridge of mountains in
Mexico is the Sierra Madre, or Mother
Mountains, for from them all other
ridges and spurs seem to emanate. From
their crests, as with all other mountains
in the world, spring innumerable rivulets
and creeks, which, uniting, form rivers.
But nearly everywhere else these streams
increase in size by the addition of the
waters of other tributaries until they reach
the sea.

Not so with the Mexican rivers of this
locality. Shortly after leaving the mountains and reaching the foothills, they receive no additions from other sources,
and after flowing from fifty to one hundred miles they sink into the ground.

These "sinks" are usually large lakes, and a map of the country would make one believe that the rivers were emptying into them, but in reality they only disappear as just stated, to reappear in the hot lands as the heads of rivers. Now all the country between the Sierra Madre and the "sinks," or at least all the valley country, can be readily irrigated by this perennial flow of water. The rivers are fringed with trees, and the grass is in excellent condition, while beyond, the plains are treeless, the soil arid, and the prospect cheerless in comparison. To particularize: if the reader looks at the map of Chihuahua he will see a series of lakes (they are the "sinks" to which I refer): Laguna de Guzman, Laguna (the Spanish for lake) de Santa Maria, Laguna de Patos, etc., extending nearly north and

south, and parallel with the crest of the
Sierra Madres. Between the lakes and
the crest is a beautiful country, capable of
sustaining a dense population ; while outside of it, to the eastward, so much cannot
be said in its favor, although probably the
latter is a good grazing district. Now
the railway runs outside or eastward of
the line of the "sinks," where the country
is flat and the engineering difficulties are
at a minimum ; and as nearly all the
descriptions we have of Mexico are based
upon observations made from car windows,
it is easy to see how erroneous an opinion
can be formed of this northern portion of
Mexico, which is so constantly, though
conscientiously, misrepresented by scores
of writers.

The first lake we came to in Mexico
was Laguna Las Palomas (the Doves),

only a few miles beyond the boundary, and to secure which Mexico was smart enough to get in the offset to which I have referred. It is, I think, the "sink" of the Mimbres River, which, as a river, lies wholly in the southwestern portion of New Mexico. It disappears, however, before it crosses the boundary, to reappear as sixty or seventy huge springs in Mexico (any one of these would be worth $20,000 to $25,000 as water is now sold in the arid districts), which drain into a beautiful lake, backed by a high sierra, the Las Palomas Mountains, altogether forming a very picturesque scene. All the country around is quite level, and thousands of acres can here be irrigated with this enormous water supply; while it can only be done by the quarter section in the Southwest on our side of the line, except, probably, in a few rare instances.

This was a favorite "stamping ground" of the more warlike bands of Apache Indians but a few years ago. The water and grass for their ponies and the game for themselves made it their veritable Garden of Eden; settlement, therefore, was out of the question until these bold marauders could be ejected with powder and lead. Not two leagues to the north the road from Deming, N. M., to Las Palomas passes over two graves of as many Apaches, killed a few years ago; while on a hill hard by can be seen three crescent-shaped heaps of stones where the great Apache chief Victorio, with three or four score warriors, made a stand against the combined forces of the United States and Mexico, which proved entirely too much for him in the resulting combat.   More worthless or meaner Indians were never driven out of a country than were the Apaches after they had found this region uninhabitable, or at least unbearable for their murderous methods of life ; and for much of the decisive action that led to this desirable end we have to thank the Mexicans.

The way the Las Palomas Mountains have of rising sheer out of a level country is quite common in this region, plainly showing that the mountains once rose from a great sea that washed their bases, and when it receded with the uplifting of this region it left the level plain to show where its flat bottom had been ages before. A fine example of this is seen in the mountains called Tres Hermanas (the Three Sisters), very near the boundary

TRES HERMANAS.

line, and but a few miles from the wagon
road leading from Deming south into old
Mexico. They form an interesting feature in the landscape as viewed from the
railway on approaching Deming, and are
the subject of an illustration by our artist.

Sometimes a single peak just gets its
head above the level plain by a few
hundred feet, while again, great ranges
extend for miles, their tops covered with
snow in the winter months. However
long that level plain may be, it always
extends without break or interruption to
the next range. A railway would have
but little trouble, so far as grades are
concerned, in getting through this country. It might be necessary to wind a
great deal to avoid hills and mountains,
but if the constructors were lavish with
rails and ties, and did not mind mileage,

the grade would be almost as simple as
building on a floor ; in fact it is the floor
of an old inland ocean.

A profile view of some of these ranges
and isolated peaks gives some very
grotesque as well as picturesque views,
and imaginative people of the Southwest
fancy they see many silhouette designs
in the crests of the mountains. Faces
seem to predominate, and especially is
Montezuma's face quite lavishly distributed over this region. I think I can
recall at least a half dozen of them in the
Southwest since I first visited there in
1867. This unfortunate Aztec monarch
must have had a very rocky looking face,
or his descendants must have thought
exceeding well of him to sculpture him
so often, even in fancy, upon the mountain crests.

I went into a little face-making business
of my own, so as to keep along in the
custom of the country while I was there.
The most southerly peak of the Florida
range had quite a well-defined face,
upturned to the sky, that, to my imagination, looked more like the well-known
face of Benjamin Franklin than any other
of nature's sculpturing so often portrayed
in mountains when assisted by the fancy
of man.

Before leaving Las Palomas our
material underwent inspection by the
customs officials, and no people could
have been more polite and considerate
than were these officers toward us, giving
us our necessary papers without putting
us to the inconvenience of unpacking our
many boxes and bundles. There is this
peculiarity about Mexican frontier cus-

toms : after passing the first one you are by no means through with them, for the next two, three, or even four towns may also have customhouse officers. I was in a Mexican town, La Ascencion, and had a wagon unloaded before I knew they had a customhouse. I expected to be shot at reveille the next morning; but instead they politely passed all my personal baggage without even asking to see it, simply examining the papers received at the first customhouse.

After leaving Las Palomas our course lay southward across a high *mesa,* or table-land, until we reached the Boca Grande River. The scenery along the Boca Grande is picturesque and somewhat peculiar. The river bottom is flat, very wide, and rich in soil; but on the flanks rise the Mexican mountains sheer

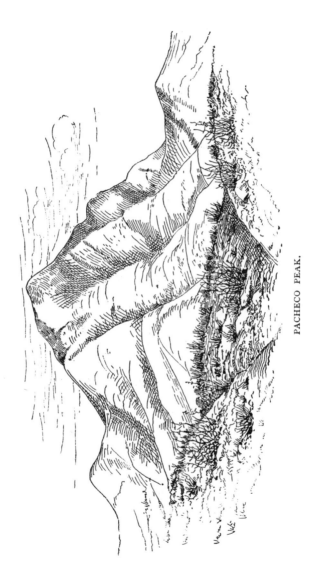

PACHECO PEAK.

out of the plains. To the west are the
Sierra Madres, covered with snow on the
highest peaks, making some of the most
beautiful views I have ever seen as presented from different points along the
river's course. One of them, Pacheco
Peak, in the Boca Grande range (named
after the Mexican Minister of the Interior), is shown in the illustration. Slight
spurs and *mesa* lands extend from the
sierras in the valleys and often reach the
river bank, thereby forcing the road over
them, but affording a foundation that any
macadamized highway in our own country might emulate. Some of these
ridges were ornamented with groupings
of cactus (of the oquetilla variety), if
their presence can be called an ornament. Imagine a dozen fishing rods,
from ten to fifteen feet in length, all

radiating from a central point like a bouquet of bayonets, and each rod holding hundreds of spikes throughout its

OQUETILLA CACTUS.

length. You will thus have a faint idea of the appearance of a bunch of oquetilla cactus. These bunches seem to prefer growing along the rocky crests in rows of tolerable regularity that, to a person at a distance, suggest the work of human hands.

We traveled some thirty miles along the river without seeing a living thing except a few jack rabbits and coyotes, when suddenly we rounded a bend of the beautiful Boca Grande and came upon a stretch of valley covered with zacaton grass, and which in a few years will be a valuable ranche. Across this we saw two as hard-looking characters approaching us as ever cut a throat. I was preparing to hand over to them all my Mexican money and other valuables when they politely touched their hats and simply said, "Documentos." Here, again, in the far-off woods and hills were more customhouse officials. These men were here to prevent smugglers from crossing the border between the towns and established highways.

We lunched that day on Espia Hill,

used formerly as a customhouse post of observation, but the Apache chief Geronimo, raiding through here, collected a poll tax of one scalp apiece, and since then the post has been abandoned. A short distance further the river changes from the Boca Grande to the Casas Grandes.

The Boca Grande and the Casas Grandes are the same river, like the Wind River and the Big Horn in our own country, the two changing names at a certain point. In other words, they have the same river bed, for in the dryest seasons the Casas Grandes sinks and reappears further down as the Boca Grande, the two streams being really identical most of the way, however, and both of them emptying into the great "sink" known as Laguna Guzman. I

noticed one peculiarity of the rocky soil
on the ridges extending down from the
foothills of the mountains that I have
never seen elsewhere, and might not have
noticed even here had it not been pointed
out to me by one of my guides. Great
areas of the soil were covered with stones,
mostly flat in shape, and so numerous
that but little vegetation could exist
between them. A decidedly desolate
aspect was thus presented; indeed no
one would believe that anything except
the oquetilla cactus could possibly grow
here. One of my Mexican men, however, assured me that the stones were
only on the surface, and that by removing
them the richest of red soil could be
found underneath, not affording a single
stone in a cubic yard of earth. The soil
had not been washed away when the rains

beat down upon it, as this "top-dressing" of flat rock had shielded it from such action, protecting it, let us hope, for the future use of man. They told me this peculiar kind was the richest and most easily cultivated soil in Mexico, but it looked, with its covering of rocks, poor enough to put in some terrestrial alms-house along with the Sahara Desert.

This whole Southwest, or rather North-west from a Mexican standpoint, is a country of deceptive appearances. Hun- dreds of my readers have probably traveled over the Santa Fé Railway as it courses through the Rio Grande valley, and, recalling the grassy, pleasant-looking country in the East, have wondered how this cheerless area of sand and sagebrush could ever be utilized. Yet in this valley is a farm of twenty-two acres for which sixty thousand dollars has been flatly refused, although not one cent of its value is due to its proximity to any important point (as the fact is with the valuable little farms around our Eastern cities), but solely to what it will produce. Verily the desolation of the land is deceptive, and, like beauty, is but skin deep.

# CHAPTER II.

NORTHWESTERN CHIHUAHUA (CONTINUED)
—MEXICAN MORMON COLONIES — FROM
LA ASCENSION TO CORRALITOS — SOME
RUINS ALONG THE TAPASITA—A TOLTEC
BABYLON.

IT is sixty to sixty-five miles from Las Palomas to La Ascension, and not a settlement or a sign of life except jack rabbits, coyotes, and customhouse officers is to be seen throughout the whole length of this unusually rich country, so effectually did the Apaches enforce their restrictive tariff but a few years ago. At rare intervals great haciendas are found in these rich valleys, the main

34

industry of which is cattle raising. We passed a herd of about a thousand head just before reaching La Ascension, all in magnificent condition, and attended by some eight or ten *vaqueros*, who were driving them to market. With the usual Mexican politeness they took particular pains to give us the road ; and to do so drove the whole herd over a high hill, around the base of which the road ran.

Just before reaching La Ascension we came to the Mormon colony of Diaz (named by them in honor of the present President of the Mexican Republic), numbering about fifty families. A discussion of their religious tenets is clearly and fortunately out of my province, not only from its heavy, dreary character, but for the reason that everything wise and otherwise about Mormonism has already been put before those who care to read it. But entirely aside from the subject of polygamy, which has so completely obscured every other point about these people, they have one characteristic which is seldom heard of in connection with them and their wanderings in the Western wilderness. I refer to their building up of new countries. They have no peer in pioneering among the Caucasian races. They are so far ahead of the Gentiles in organized and discriminating, businesslike colonization, that the latter are not close enough to them to permit a comparison that would show their inferiority. Of course they (the Mormons) see in their belief an ample explanation for this excellence; it is far more probable, however, as I look at it from my Gentile point of view, that it is due to the peculiar organization of their Church, which so fits them for the work of making the wilderness blossom as the rose.

No other Christian Church exercises so much authority over the temporal affairs of its members as the Mormon Church. However debatable this exercise of authority may be in civilized communities, surrounded by people of the same kind, there is no doubt in my mind as to its favorable effect upon pioneer associations, encompassed by enemies in man and nature. This view of the subject must be admitted by everyone who has grown up on the Gentile frontier and seen the innumerable bickerings between adjacent towns, the internal dissensions in the towns themselves, the rivalry for "booms," the shotgun contests for county seats, the thousands of exaggerations about their own interests, and the hundreds of depreciations about those of others adjoining. As in its spiritual, so in its temporal affairs, the authority of the Mormon Church is remarkable for its effective power of centralization. It judicially settles all questions for the general, not the individual good; and upon this principle it determines, by the character of the soil, and by the natural routes of travel, where colonies shall locate, as well as what are the probable opportunities for propagation of the faith. It is not at all surprising to one who has observed these facts that an organized faith of almost any character should have flourished, though surrounded by so much disorganization.

As a rule, at least from two to four years of quiet are needed after an Indian

war to restore such confidence among
the whites that they can settle the disturbed district in a *bona-fide* way. I
should, however, except the Mormons
from this class, but to do so without
an explanation would appear somewhat
unreasonable. Their long and almost
constant frontier experience has taught
them how to weigh Indian matters cor-
rectly, as well as others pertaining to the
ragged edge of civilization. Although
the Apaches had been subdued a dozen
times by the Mexican and American
governments alternately, they knew
when the subduing meant subjugation,
and before Geronimo and his cabinet
were halfway to the orange groves of
Florida, Mormon wagon poles were
pointing to the rich valleys of Northwestern Chihuahua.

They number here a few hundred families, a mere fraction in view of all the available land of the magnificent valleys of the Casas Grandes, Boca Grande, Santa Maria, and others ; and they never will predominate politically or in numbers over the other inhabitants if we include the Mexican population, which is almost universally Catholic. In fact, those already established seem content merely to settle down and be let alone ; this end they attain by purchase of tracts of land over which they can throw their authority and be a little community unto themselves, neither disturbing nor wishing to be disturbed by others.

Their success has already invited the more avaricious, but less coldly calculating Gentile ; and while it is stating it a little strong to say there is a " boom," or even indications of one, within the thirty to sixty miles between villages, my conscience is not disturbed in saying that I can at least agree with the great American poet that,

> We hear the first low wash of waves
> Where soon shall roll a human sea.

Already a railway was talked of, and the usual undue excitement was manifested. Every stranger was supposed to have something to do with it. Even my own little expedition was thought to be a sort of preliminary reconnoissance. I have never constructed a railway in my life, but I have been along the advancing lines of a number of new ones, and have seen them grow from two iron rails in a wilderness to a great country. I do not recall any that had much brighter prospects ahead than the proposed one along the eastern slopes of the Sierra Madres. That it must be built some day the resources of the country clearly demand, and it is to be hoped that it will be at as early a date as possible.

At La Ascension we were greatly indebted to Mr. Francis, a young English gentleman, who literally placed his house at our disposal, giving up his own room for our comfort. As there were no inns in La Ascension except those of the lowest order, this generous hospitality of the only Englishman in the town was warmly appreciated by us. One of our wagons having met with a slight accident, we remained over Sunday to await repairs. As soon as this was known to the inhabitants invitations began to pour in to attend cockfights, and one of especial magnitude

was organized in our honor. The finest
cocks in the place were to take part, and
the *presidente* or mayor of the town would
preside. Then, to add distinction to the
already exciting programme, a *baile* or ball
was hastily gotten up for the evening.
Hospitality could go no farther in this
out-of-the-way town, for the people were
really not rich enough to support a bull-
fight. Early in the morning, before the
population had recovered from the dissipa-
tions of the previous night, we bade our
hospitable host "good-by," and, wrapped
in our heaviest coats against the chill
morning air, we started southward toward
Corralitos, about thirty-five or forty miles
away. After crossing wide *mesas* and
threading our way around the bases of
many picturesque groups of mountains,
we came to the Casas Grandes River and

valley, and along this stream, literally alive with ducks, we traveled for some hours. It was a great temptation to get out the guns and shoot at the ducks that were calmly sailing by us on the broad and rapid stream; but as we had neither dog nor boat it would have been impossible to secure them had we done so. The consoling thought was ours that the hacienda was not far distant, and there we would likely find everything necessary to assist us in this or any other sport.

Approaching the hacienda we passed immense droves of horses and cattle grazing on the rich bottom lands. Corralitos has a very pretty, an almost poetical name, but it loses much of its romantic character when it is known that it is named for some old, dilapidated sheep pens that once existed here, corralitos being little pens or little corrals. It is a hacienda, some eighty or ninety years old, with an extremely interesting history, that would make a book more thrilling than any fiction. The main building is a great square inclosure with very thick walls, having many loopholes for guns, and high turrets or towers at the corners. To enter the building are massive gates, while inside are a number of courts with other gates leading to other inclosures, and making the interior building appear like a small town. Here during the fierce Apache raids the whole population was gathered for protection, and the crack of Apache rifles has often been heard around the thick walls. Dons of Spanish blood have extracted fortunes from the mountain sides near by in mines that have been worked since shortly after the Conquest.

It is a hacienda of about a million acres in extent, and one of the most beautiful in the whole State of Chihuahua, the Casas Grandes River running for some thirty miles through the estate. The true hacienda, of which we hear so much in Mexican narration, is really a definite area of twenty-two thousand acres, but the name is now used so as to mean almost any estate, whether large or small, under one management. With the advance of railways haciendas are slowly disappearing, and will soon exist only in poetry or fiction.

The views from the hacienda are beautiful in the extreme. To the east lies a range of mountains filled with seams of silver, the Corralitos Company working some thirty to forty mines; while one hundred and fifty to two hundred " pros-

pects" await development. These mines
have been known and worked since the
Spaniards entered this part of Mexico.
To the west of the hacienda flows the
Casas Grandes River, flanked on either
side by enormous old cottonwood trees;
while for a background rise the immense
peaks of the Sierra Madres, covered with
snow, and breaking into all sorts of fantastic shapes as they extend down toward
the river.

The Corralitos Company is owned
mainly in the United States, New York
capitalists being the principal stock-
holders.

While at Diaz City I had learned from
Dr. W. Derby Johnson, the ecclesiastical
head of the Mormon colonies in Upper
Chihuahua, that at the lower colony on
the Piedras Verdes River a number of

ancient Aztec ruins were to be seen, very few of which had ever been heard of before. I determined to visit them as soon as possible, for the reason that Mr. Macdonald, the business manager of the lower colony, was expecting to leave shortly for Salt Lake City. This gentleman was unusually well acquainted with the country of the Piedras Verdes, having spent months in surveying it, and being more familiar with its ancient ruins than any other man living. Fortunately Dr. Johnson was going through to see him— a two days' trip—so to a certain extent we joined our forces for that time. Expecting to return to Corralitos, we left early one morning for a drive of about sixty miles to the lower Mormon colony of Juarez, named after Mexico's greatest President since the war of independence.

Twenty-five or thirty miles to the south of Corralitos we came to the town of Casas Grandes, said to consist of three thousand inhabitants, but we did not see three people as we drove through its seemingly deserted streets. It is the most important town in the valley, both historically and in point of numbers. It takes its name, meaning "big houses," from the ancient ruins situated in its suburbs, and comprising the largest found in this part of Mexico when it was first visited by Europeans many years ago. The name of the town has also been applied to the river which flows just in front of it, and which is formed by the junction of two others, the San Miguel and Piedras Verdes. The San Miguel is the straight line prolongation of the Casas Grandes, and is apparently

the true stream ; but the Piedras Verdes
is the more important, as its waters are
perennially replenished by branches
which rise in the never-failing springs
of the sierras to the west. At Casas
Grandes we left the river and struck out
inland for the little Mormon colony on
the Piedras Verdes River, a distance of
some twenty or twenty-five miles. Like
all other distances in this part of Mexico, there is not a sign of civilization
between, not even a camping place, although the country traversed is a fine
one for cattle grazing, with numerous
beautiful valleys where farms could be
made remunerative, and where three or
four dozen houses ought to be seen if
a tenth part of the country's resources
were developed. As we crossed stretch
after stretch of beautiful prairie, watered

by many little mountain streams, it
seemed as though only a short time must
pass before this fertile country would be
dotted with hundreds of homes and
thousands of cattle on its grassy hills.
The meaning of Piedras Verdes is green
rocks, but the rock projections in cliff,
hill, or stream, are of all imaginable
shades, not only of green, but of red,
yellow, brown, rose, and even blue. The
effect is inconceivably beautiful against
the wonderful blue sky of this part
of Mexico. Just before reaching the
Mormon colony you come to a high
ridge from which can be seen the little
town nestling along the banks of the picturesque Piedras Verdes River. It is a
scene seldom surpassed in beauty. Far
to the west are the grand Sierra Madres,
crested with snow, while nearer, the

great shaggy hills, covered with timber,
and the many bright-colored rocks between, make up a picture that neither
poet nor painter could depict.

Juarez is a bright-looking little town of
some fifty families, who raise all their own
fruits and vegetables, and have a goodly
supply for the less thrifty people of the
surrounding country.   Our party was
kindly cared for by two or three of the
Mormon families, as there were no other
places of shelter beside their homes.
The next day we started to visit the
ancient ruins on the Tapasita River (a
branch of the Piedras Verdes), which
flows through as beautiful a little valley
as I ever saw.   Mr. Macdonald, the surveyor of this tract, kindly consented to
accompany us, although he was overbur-
dened with business incidental to starting

the next day for Salt Lake City. In the
Tapasita valley I expected to find only a
single well-defined group of ruins. Imagine my surprise, then, upon discovering
that the entire country, especially in its
valleys, was covered with such evidences.
A high hill, called the Picacho de Torreon,
had been occupied on its southern face by
cliff dwellers ; at our feet was a mass of
rubbish that indicated a ruin of the latter
people. Twelve miles up the Tapasita
was still another extensive ruin of stone,
while the intervening space was constantly
marked by similar remains. In fact, as
before stated, the whole valley was one
vast continuation of ruins. We were
surely on ground once occupied by
an ancient and dense population—where
the fertile resources of the country will
again sustain another and a far more civ-

ilized race.  Even Juarez City found a
great many such mounds on its site, and
digging into some of them has revealed
much of interest.   Just before our arrival
a pot or jar had been taken from one of

ANCIENT JAR UNEARTHED AT JUAREZ CITY.

the mounds, and was bought by me of the
young boy who unearthed it.   It is like
many other jars from Casas Grandes, as
well as from better known ruins, and that
have already figured in works on Mexico.
It differs, however, from most of them in
having upon it the figure of a bird, as

representations of animals of any sort are
very unusual upon their decorated sur-
faces. The bird seems more nearly to
resemble the chaparral cock or California
road runner than any other bird in this
part of the world. Geometrical designs
are frequent, and of these the zigzag,
stairlike forms are the most common.
Many other things had been found in this
mound, including a number of utensils of
pottery, together with the human bones
of their makers. No doubt similar relics,
with some variations, could be found in
all these mounds. We saw, I think, many
hundreds of these ruins in the Piedras
Verdes region, most of them merely
mounds suggestive of what they once
were. Ancient ditches could also be
plainly made out along the hillsides,
showing that the former inhabitants cul-

tivated the rich soil of the valleys. They well understood the value of water, too, for around the bases of the small, stream-less valleys leading into the watered ones were damlike terraces, evidently designed to catch and retain the water after show-ers until it was needed in the irrigating ditches. On the top of high hills adja-cent were fortified places, apparently where they must have fled in times of danger from other tribes. They were a wonderful and interesting people, one that would repay careful study, even from the little evidence of their existence that is left.

On the Tapasita we came upon the ruins of what must have been a large city of these people—the largest we saw in that part of the country. The only life we saw there was a mountain lion or panther, that came trotting along the valley until it saw us, when it turned back into the mountains. Truly the wild beasts were wandering over the Toltec Babylon.

It is impossible for an artist to convey in plain black and white any idea of the beauty of this country ; it is a land requiring the painter to exhibit its beauties.

One of the interesting peculiarities of the numerous ruins found throughout this portion of the country, and that indicates a once dense population living off the soil, is the way in which most of them seem to have met their fate. When a ruined house is dug into all the skeletons of its occupants are found in what may be termed the combined kitchen and eating room,—these two

rooms being in one,—and always near a
fire-place. The postures of these skeletons are as various as it is possible for
the human body to assume. They are
found kneeling, stretched out, sometimes
with their locked hands over their heads,
on their sides, and, again, with their children in their arms, hardly any two being
alike in the same house or series of
houses, where they were united into a
pueblo. Now in the whole study of sep-
ulture it has been almost universally
found that even among the lowest savages as well as among the most civilized
peoples, whatever form of burial is
adopted, no matter how absurd from our
point of view, it is uniform in the main
points, allowing, of course, slight devia-
tions for caste or rank. The positions
of the skeletons in their own houses do

not accord with this general fact, and
have led some to believe that this race
was destroyed by an earthquake or other
violent action of nature.

I had a long talk with Mr. Davis,
superintendent of the Corralitos Company, who has made a study of these
ancient ruins from having them almost
forced upon his attention. That gentleman not only believes they were cut off
by a violent earthquake, as I have sug-
gested, but that this great cataclysm
caught them at their evening meal. He
infers the latter fact from a consideration
of the customs of the present almost pure-
blooded Indians here, who must have
descended from the older race, although,
singularly enough, knowing nothing of
their ancient progenitors. The evening
meal is the only occasion when they are

all gathered together at home. The
earthquake must have been a very severe
one, and have brought down the large
buildings upon the occupants before they
could escape. This region is not especially liable to such disasters. That it
has them, however, occasionally, and
severe ones too, is shown by the Bavispe
earthquake of a few years ago, when that
town was destroyed, some forty people
killed, and the whole country shaken up.
Mr. Davis goes on with his theory that
the survivors were thus exposed to the
mercy of their enemies (that they had
enemies before is shown by their fortifications adjoining almost every village),
and became cliff dwellers as a last resource
to escape the fury of their old assailants.
These, probably, were savages by comparison ; and, living in savage homes, as

skin tents or *wikeyups,* and other light
abodes, they suffered little from the great
commotion referred to. When the par-
tially vanquished race became strong
enough they wandered southward as the
first, or among the first, Toltec excursions
in that direction.

While at Corralitos Mr. Davis told
me of some ruins situated about halfway between his hacienda and Casas
Grandes, near Barranca. I visited them
next day, and found a very noticeable
and well-defined road leading straight up
a hill to a slight bench overtopped by a
higher hill at the end of the bench.
Here was an ancient ruin, built of stone,
and looking very much like a position of
defense. It may have been a sacrificial
place, for otherwise I cannot account for
the careful construction of the road.

For defensive purposes it would not
have been needed, especially one so well
made ; but observation has taught me
that, when no other reasonable explanation can be found for doing a thing,
superstitious or religious motives can be
consistently introduced to account for it.
This hill was really an outlying one from
a larger near by and overlooking it.
After climbing up the latter about halfway a series of stone buildings, not dis-
cernible from the bottom, were clearly
made out.  They encircled the hill, and
about halfway between these and the
top of the hill was another row of encir-
cling buildings, faintly recognized by
their ruins, although the masonry was of
the best character.  On the top of the
hill was a fortification, with a well probably about twenty feet from the summit,

overtopped and almost hidden by a hang-
ing mesquite bush. At the base of both
hills was a series of mounds extending as
far as the eye could reach. I almost
fear to place an estimate on their number, nor can I positively say they repre-
sented buildings at all. In all or nearly
all other mounds there is some sign of
the house walls protruding through the
*débris ;* here I found none, but they
closely resemble the other mounds except in this respect. Everything goes to
show that these people were on the defensive, and that defense was often necessary. The ruins looked very much older
than any others I had visited, but that
can in a measure be accounted for, I
think, by the sandy character of the district. Nothing makes an abandoned
building or other work of man look so

antiquated as drifting sand piled up around it. This town, therefore, may have been contemporaneous with the ruined towns of the Casas Grandes valley generally, although the latter look much more recent from being built on more compact soil.

As I have already more than hinted, all these valleys along the foothills of the Sierra Madre Mountains may have held a dense population when these ancient people sojourned here, and if the physical characteristics were the same as at the present time it is very easy to account for. To the westward it is too mountainous for many people to find homes and cultivate the soil, while to the eastward the country is too barren after one passes the line of the lakes, or where the mountain rivers sink.

The strip along the foothills, between
the main ridge of mountains and the
plains, is about the only place where
an agricultural people could live in large
numbers and thrive ; and now that the
dreaded Apache Indian has been finally
subdued, I think the day is not far distant when it will be again peopled by a
community engaged in peaceful pursuits.
These ancients probably raised everything they needed, so that there was
very little commerce between them, and
not much need of roads or trails,
although a few of them are occasionally
made out with great distinctness.

I have already spoken of the plainly
marked road leading up the steep sides
of Davis Hill. One can see this fully a
mile away, although not able to fully
make out its true character at that dis-

tance; the observer might suppose it to be a strip of light grass in a depression, until his error was corrected by a closer inspection.

The fortifications on the summit, considered from a military standpoint, were the most complete that could be desired. The hills retreated on both sides, giving full scope to the eye up and down the broad valley, every square yard of which was probably irrigated and cultivated. Without doubt the fortifications could safely be left unguarded in clear weather, when the inhabitants would probably be at work on their farms. A few keen-sighted sentinels, suitably posted, might give notice of a coming foe in ample time for the population to man the intrenchments before an attack could possibly be made by the most rapidly moving enemy. This, of course, assumes that the able-bodied citizen of that day was equally an artisan or farmer and a soldier; it is an assumption, however, that accords with our knowledge of many other ancient races.

On our way back to the hacienda from these ruins we passed through an old, abandoned Mexican mining town called Barranca. It plainly showed its ancient character in the long rows of slag that had come from the adobe furnaces, some of which were still standing.

Although many of the adobe houses were in excellent condition, even the old church being in a fair state of preservation, there was not a soul about the place. The primitive methods of doing the work and the richness of the ore which had been smelted could be seen in any piece of slag taken from the piles. By cutting a little almost pure lead and silver were revealed, probably in the same proportions as they existed in the vein. These piles of slag would represent a fortune, with new and improved machinery like that employed in the United States, to resmelt them, and with a railway running near. This place, moreover, is only one of the many where fortunes are lying dormant in the different slag piles of the old mines of northwestern Chihuahua alone.

It is difficult to get information from the natives regarding the mineral wealth of the country. If they have a good mine they are exceedingly shy about saying so, and they are very jealous lest foreigners should obtain valuable mining property. They dislike to see it pass from under

their control, and do not take kindly to
the foreign spirit of enterprise and
improvement. This, however, is quite
contrary to the policy of the Mexican
Government, which is doing all it can to
induce capital to come in for investment.
The country is in a stable, settled condition, and we found every part that we
visited quite as safe as the more settled
communities of the United States. The
politeness and disposition to oblige of
the humblest of the Mexican people you
can rely upon invariably, and that is
more than can be said of the corresponding class in more enlightened
countries.

This day of our visit to the ruins of
Davis Hill was very warm, and our
driver, not having a taste for antiquarian
research, even in the modest degree pos-

sessed by me, had quite resented being dragged from the shade of the great cottonwood trees around the hacienda. To show his native independence of spirit he therefore refused to listen to advice and water his horses on the road, but on returning allowed them to drink all they wanted ; as a consequence one horse died. We left Deming with two large American horses, but now found it impossible, even on that great hacienda, to obtain a suitable match, so we were obliged to start off with a comical, sturdy broncho for a mate, which not only gave a very lop-sided look to the conveyance, but an appearance of extreme cruelty toward the little animal. Whenever the big horse trotted the little fellow would take up a canter to keep alongside, and it was almost enough to make a person

seasick to watch the ill-mated pair get
over the ground.

We were soon back again to Corralitos,
and inside the forbidding looking gates.
Here we were very comfortably housed,
with a bright fire burning in the bedroom
fireplace to take the chill off the air, as
the rooms in these thick adobe buildings
are much like cellars in their temperature,
whether it is warm or cold outside. We
had not been in many hours before other
strangers began to arrive : Englishmen
from their ranches, miners from the silver
mines, a surveying party, and a number of
cattlemen. By nightfall the place was
swarming with people, and the problem
was where to stow away so many for the
night. The long table in the old adobe
dining room was three times full. There
is no lack of fresh meat on such an haci-

enda, all that is necessary being to send out the butcher, who kills whatever is wanted from the abundant supply on the range, for in that clear, rare atmosphere meat is preserved until used.

There is another feature of large haciendas like this that may prove interesting. I refer to the store, which usually occupies one corner of the building. At this store is found every kind of merchandise that is wanted, and here is doled out to the Indian population in exchange for their work certain quantities of flour or sugar,—you can be sure the amount is always very small,—and in time the simple people draw much more than is due them for work, as they are always allowed credit. Then it is they become peons or slaves, for they rarely get out of debt, but increase it until they are virtually owned

by the lords of the soil, who can do as
they please with the poor creatures, and
work them whenever and wherever they
see fit. These debts descend from father
to son ; in this manner they are continually increasing, and so the chains are riv-
eted. I suppose the system has many
advantages as well as disadvantages, but
certainly we see the disadvantages to the
poor and simple people, who, having their
immediate wants supplied, do not care to
look beyond. Among the more intelligent this condition is very galling, but as
a rule they are shrewd enough to avoid it.

Standing a short distance from the
inclosing wall of the hacienda, and in the
midst of the poor quarter, was a dilapidated Roman Catholic church. There
was no resident priest, but one came twice
a year from a settlement farther south.

At all hours of the day, however, women could be found kneeling in front of the primitive altar, a poor, degraded class, with not as much morality as the most savage tribes who have never heard of civilization.

My trip of over two hundred miles down the eastern slope of the Sierra Madre Mountains, from the boundary between the two countries, coupled with the information I gained *en route*, showed me that I might do better by attempting to make my way through the great range from the westward ; so it was decided to make the change of base from the State of Chihuahua to that of Sonora.

While visiting at La Ascension on our return trip we saw about a dozen Mexicans extracting silver from ore by a method which is as old as that mentioned

in the Bible. The rich ore, showing
probably two hundred and fifty dollars
to the ton, had been taken out of
the vein with crowbars and by rough
blasting, and then brought to the town on
the backs of burros. Here the huge rocks
were first crushed with sledge hammers
until they were about the size of one's fist
and could be easily handled, then broken
again with smaller hand hammers until
almost as fine as coarse sand. This was
reduced to a complete powder by being
beaten in heavy leather bags. After these
operations it was mixed with water and
thrown into an *arastra*, a cross between a
coffee mill and a quartz crusher ; in other
words, consisting of four stones tied to a
revolving mill-bar and turned by the inev-
itable mule. This makes a paste rich in
granulated silver, which is mixed with salt

and boiled in a little pot, as if they were making apple butter instead of working one of the richest veins of silver in a country celebrated for its valuable silver mines. The resulting mass is washed out in a pan, as a prospecting miner washes for signs of gold, with the exception that quicksilver is put in to form an amalgam with the now liberated metal. The latter is pressed out with the hand, and the little ball of amalgam, as bright as silver itself, has the mercury driven off by a furnace only big enough to fry the eggs for a party of two. The pure silver ball, glistening like hoar frost in the sun, is now beaten down to the size of a big marble to prevent its breaking to pieces. It is exasperating in the extreme to see such ignorant methods of man applied to the rich offerings of nature.

There was but very little out of the usual routine of travel for a day or two, until we came to the third crossing of the Casas Grandes River, at a point so near its entrance into Laguna Guzman that we felt sure we would have no trouble in getting over. For, as I have already explained, most of the rivers in this country are larger the nearer you approach their heads. There had been no rains to swell the streams, and our surprise can therefore be imagined when, upon reaching the river, we found it a raging torrent. A long experience had taught me that it does not pay to await the falling of a swollen river; so we set at work to get over the obstreperous stream. The loads were all piled on the seats, above the empty wagon beds, which, being thus weighted and top-heavy, acted

like so many boats when they dashed
into the river. Our driver, a Mexican,
had the worst of it in a low, light wagon,

CROSSING THE CASAS GRANDES RIVER.

drawn by two small pinto bronchos. The
flood swept him down stream under an
overhanging clump of willows, despite a
rope tied to the tongue of the wagon and
another held firmly by a half dozen persons on the upstream side. But he was
as cool at the head as at the feet, although he was knee deep in ice water at

the time as he stood up in the wagon bed.
After waiting a moment to allow the
horses to regain their bewildered senses,
he swam them upstream to the crossing,
and the men, with a whoop and a yell,
dragged the whole affair on shore, looking like drowned rats tied to a cigar box.
We were three hours and a quarter
getting over that river, and felt as if we
could have drowned the man who wrote
that Northern Mexico is a vast, waterless
tract of country.

# CHAPTER III.

FROM Deming, N. M., it is but a five
or six hours' ride by rail to Benson in
Arizona, the initial point of the Sonora
railway, a branch of the Atchison, Topeka, and Santa Fé, and extending to
the seaport of Guaymas in Mexico. The
ride from Benson consumes two days,
and the route is through the mountains,
down the lovely, fertile valleys, and
across the flat, tropical country of the
seacoast. It is a ride of great novelty

and of surpassing beauty throughout the
entire distance. After the train reached
Nogalles, a town which is half in the
United States and half in Mexico, it was
made up in regular Mexican fashion of
first, second, and third class coaches;
and, from the number of Mexicans
aboard, it appeared they were as much
given to travel as their more active
neighbors of the North; with this difference, however : that where they can save
a penny by going second or third class
they do so. This fact removes an interesting feature of Mexican travel from the
sight of the average American tourist,
for, as a rule, he prefers comfort to the
study of the picturesque in his fellow-
travelers.

When we reached Hermosillo, a place
of about ten thousand people, the sta-

tion was filled with vendors of oranges; and such oranges I never tasted elsewhere, although I have sampled that fruit in some of the most famous groves of Florida and California. In sweetness, delicious flavor, and juiciness they surpass all others; in fact it is impossible to find a poor or insipid one among all you can buy and eat. It is a pity there is so little market for this very superior fruit. The entire country from Hermosillo down to the coast seems to be a perfect one for orange culture, and for all other semi-tropical fruits. The prices paid for oranges are very reasonable, for much more is grown than can be consumed, and there seems to be little outlet for the surplus in any direction.

Just before reaching Guaymas the railway winds among the coast range of

mountains, and crosses a shallow arm of
the sea that is bridged with a long trestle.
As you pass over the bridge you can
look across the harbor through the gaps
in the steep mountains straight out to
sea, or rather into the Gulf of California.
Again you are treated to long vistas of
the beautiful mountain-locked harbor as
the train winds around the steep peaks
and you approach the old seaport. Before going to this port, the principal one
on the Gulf of California, I made up my
mind there would be comparatively little
to say regarding it, as it is not only the
terminus of a railway, but is also located
on one or two lines of steamship travel,
and would therefore be almost as well
known as some California resorts or
other famous places of the Pacific coast.
It proved, on the contrary, to be seldom

or never visited by tourists. I could find nothing about it in my numerous guide-books and volumes devoted to Mexico, but nevertheless discovered a great deal of interest in this typical old town that was both novel and attractive. When the Sonora railway first reached here a number of years ago everything was ready to be "boomed." A hotel to cost a quarter of a million was started on a beautiful knoll overlooking the pictur-esque harbor, but after about one-tenth that amount had been put into the foun-dation and carriage way leading up the hill it was given up.

It may not be inappropriate to say that all of Guaymas is very much like the hotel—it has a fine foundation, but not much of anything else, although its sanitary conditions for a winter resort

are nowhere else excelled. The first day
you arrive you get a sample of the
weather in mild, warm days, with cool
nights, that will not vary a hair's breadth
in all your stay. The harbor is picturesque in the extreme. It is completely
landlocked, and swarms with a hundred
kinds of fishes. It looks not unlike the
harbor of San Francisco, and, although
smaller, is far more interesting in the
many beautiful vistas it opens to sight as
one sails over its intricate waters. If it
should ever become a popular winter
resort no finer fishing or sailing could be
had than in the harbor of Guaymas and
the Gulf of California. A constant sea
or land breeze is blowing in summer and
winter, but it is never strong enough to
make the waters dangerous. I have
been fishing several times, and certainly

the piscatorial bill of fare, as shown by my experience, has been an extremely varied one.

While off the shore in the harbor one afternoon I caught a shark measuring a little over six feet in length, which gave me a tussle of about a quarter of an hour before I could pull it alongside and plunge a knife into its heart. This last operation, be it observed, was not so much to end its own sufferings as to prevent those of other and better fish, and maybe a human being or so, in the near future. The natives told me, however, that it was only the large spotted or tiger shark, a species seldom seen there, that will deign to mistake the leg of a swimmer for the early worm that is caught by the bird. None of the shark kind enter the inner harbor where a sen-

A VIEW OF GUAYMAS HARBOR.

sible person would naturally bathe, as he wants enough water to hide his move-ments from his prey, and this condition seldom exists in the inner harbor. In-deed its name, Guaymas, borrowed from that of an Indian tribe, means a cup of water; and it is aptly applied, for the harbor is so landlocked and protected that seldom more than the slightest rip-ple disturbs its mirror-like surface, al-though breezes that will waft sailboats prevail throughout the day.

As a further part of my fishing experi-ence we caught a number of perch-like fish called by the people *cabrilla* (mean-ing little goat-fish, on account of some fancied resemblance to that animal, so numerous in the settled parts of Mexico), and which is pronounced the sweetest fish known on the Pacific coast. They are not as big as one's hand, and, of course, it takes a great many of them to make a mess for a few persons, but once a mess is secured it cannot be equaled in all the catches known to the piscatorial art. Another fish that we secured, and which the natives call *boca dulce* (sweet mouth), looked like a German carp. It had a pale blue head, weighed from two to four pounds, and seemed to run in schools, with no truants whatever to be found outside the school. One might fish a day for the *boca dulce* and never get a bite, but on the instant one was caught you could haul them in over the side of the boat as fast as you could bait and drop your hook, the biting ceasing as suddenly as it began. They are a delicious fish for eating, and should Guaymas ever become the large-sized city which its favorable position seems to promise, the *boca dulce* will furnish one of the leading fishes for its market.

While we were there the United States Fish Commission steamer *Albatross* came into the harbor from a long cruise in investigating the fishes of the Gulf of California, and Captain Tanner of the United States Navy told a small party of us that there were enough fish in the Gulf of California to supply all the markets of Mexico and the United States. Singularly enough, nearly all this great fish supply in the Gulf was along the eastern coast of this American Adriatic, or on the Sonora and Sinaloa side, rather than on or along the coast of Lower California. A good system of railways to the interior mining camps is needed to make this great supply available to the wealth of this naturally wealthy, but now poorly developed country. This will inevitably come, for no one can travel in Northern Mexico without clearly seeing it has a grand and wonderful future ahead, that will greatly strengthen us if we are in the ascendant, and that can correspondingly hurt us in an hour of need if we are not. The tide is rapidly setting in our favor, if we take proper advantage of it.

When I first sailed on the waters of the Gulf of California, some eighteen years ago, its commerce, although small indeed, was three-fourths in the hands of Europeans, while to-day three-fourths of it is American, and only the other fourth European. We labor under one disadvantage, however, and that is we do not attempt to cater to another's taste, even though to do so would be money in our pockets. There are peculiar lines of cheap prints and cottons made in Europe that are sold only on the west coast of Mexico, not a yard finding its way to any other part of the world. Now, while our goods command higher prices, and a great deal finds a market there, it does not "exactly fill the bill," and Americans, probably from not knowing the real wants of these people, do not manufacture the needed articles, and drive foreign stuff from the Mexican market. The ignorance of our people as to the commercial value of Mexico, and especially those parts off the principal lines of railway, is certainly great, and is losing us money now, and a more important influence later. Our enormous advantage of contiguity is pressing us forward in spite of ourselves, and we ought to sweep nearly every line of commerce in Mexico from the hands of foreigners—a fact that is most emphatically true of the northern part of that rich territory.

After cooking our lunch of *cabrillas* and *boca dulces* on the northern or inside shore of San Vincente Island we made a visit to the caves on the southern or seaward face of the same island. This led us through a little gorge between two high, beetling cliffs, into which the sea had excavated the caves we were to see. Through, or rather under, this gorge the waters pour into a small underground funnel of the solid rock before they reach the little lagoon beyond. At all hours the reverberation of the rushing tide is like thunder, as it beats backward and forward in its prison. The upper crust of the funnel is pierced with occasional holes

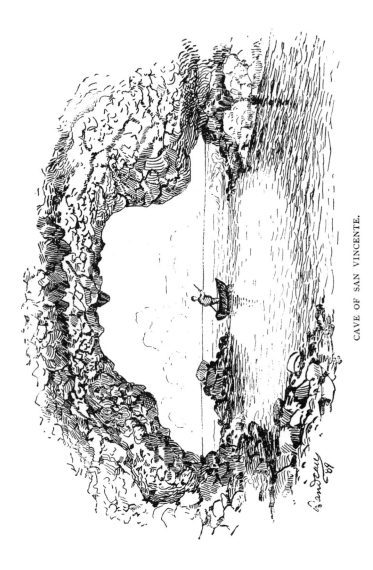

CAVE OF SAN VINCENTE.

and crevices, and at certain stages of
water these are the mouths of so many
spouting geysers, as each wave comes in
and beats against the stone roof that con-
fines it.   Woe to the person who tries to
cross just as a high wave reaches its max-
imum strength in the cave beneath ! He
will get the quickest and most effectual
bath of his lifetime.   Once on the seaward face a long line of caves is presented
to view.

The high hills here are hard conglom-
erate, and the waves of the Gulf of California, as we call it (the Gulf of Cortez
as it was first named, and is yet called by
most Mexicans), have cut far under the
cliffs, leaving overhanging masses of
rock, sometimes hundreds of feet in
depth, as measured along the roofs under
which we walked.   They looked forbid-

ding enough, and we feared that a few hundred tons might at any moment fall on our heads; for here and there could be seen just such deposits in the shallow waters, while occasional islands were discerned along the front of some of the caves which must have been formed when greater masses fell. But these fallings were without doubt centuries apart, and all these caves fully as safe to explore as caves in general. At any rate, every thought of danger was soon lost in the delicious coolness; for the day on the shining water and white sand beach had been very warm, although we hardly noticed it in the excitement of our sport. The coloring in the largest cave was beautiful beyond description. The sketch of our artist is as good as black and white can make it; but it conveys little idea of the reality, save form and contour. There was a narrow ledge on the skirts of the cave where one could find a way to enter, except at the highest tide or when a storm was beating landward, which is seldom the case, and never known during the winter months.

Guaymas has a wealth of natural attractions for the winter visitor or traveler, but hardly any reared by the hand of man to make his stay agreeable in a strictly physical sense. The hotels are all Mexican, and while they should be judged from that standpoint, probably to an American they would be very uncomfortable. Our hotel was a curious compound of saloon, kitchen, dining room, and court, all in one, with sleeping rooms ranged along two sides. One end of the building opened on a street, and the other directly on the beautiful bay, within a stone's throw of the water. The views in all directions from the water front of that simple hotel were indescribably lovely, causing one to forget the discomforts of the interior and the lack of cleanly food.

Even the inhabitants, in their Nazarene primitiveness, are very interesting. Although Guaymas claims seven thousand within her gates, her waterworks are of the same character as those of the ancient Egyptians. The chief description I shall give of them is a picture of one of the public wells just in the suburbs of the town. The water from these wells is used only for sprinkling the streets, and for household purposes, such as washing, it being totally unfit for drinking. That precious fluid is brought from a spring

ONE OF THE WELLS OF GUAYMAS.

fully seven miles back in the mountains. We were told that this water could be easily piped into the town, and that there was some talk of an attempt to do so, for the sleepy old place is beginning to awaken to the fact that the world is moving ahead.

Near the town is a sort of pleasure garden, or ranch, as it is sometimes called. It is owned by an industrious German, who sank a number of wells on the place, and obtained warm, cold, and mineral waters, and established baths, which are very popular with the people and make the place quite a resort. There are groves of all kinds of tropical fruits and plants, with flowers in the greatest profusion ; the brilliant, gorgeous flowers of the tropics growing beside the more modest ones of the temperate zone, and making the arid, rocky region beautiful with blossoms and shade. During the rainy season this country is the home of the tarantula, the centipede, and the scorpion, for they flourish equally as well as the flowers.

In one of the rooms of the American Consulate, facing the principal plaza, is lodged a piece of a shell, thrown there, singularly enough, by an American man-of-war when Guaymas was taken in 1847, during the Mexican War. At that time the *Portsmouth* and the *Congress* entered the harbor, shelled the town, and took it. The piece of shell referred to lodged in the huge wooden rafters of the building, and as these are never covered in the simple architecture of that country its rusty, round side is plainly visible from beneath. From the positions assigned to the vessels it is said to have been the *Congress,* she of *Monitor-Merrimac* fame afterward; and as the American flag still floats from the staff directly over the shell it is quite an interesting and historic piece of iron. Very few Americans, however, associate the quiet little town of Guaymas with any event of the war waged so long ago that its memories are almost lost in the later and greater war of civil strife.

In the good old times Guaymas used to have revolutions of its own. Whenever a governor of the place was financially embarrassed, or imagined he would soon be replaced by some fresh favorite from the City of Mexico, he would issue a proclamation and send around to merchant after merchant to take up a collection. If they had the temerity to object, not wishing to part with their worldly goods in that fashion, one of their number was selected as an example, taken out and shot, which had the desired effect of causing the others to come to time. We had the pleasure of meeting one of the old-time governors who had ruled in this fashion. He now holds an important position, is a man of great wealth, and a distinguished citizen—a tall, fine-looking man—but I could not help thinking he looked the born pirate, and would enjoy playing the despot again if he had the opportunity.

The great mass of the working class of this western part of Mexico are the Yaqui and Mayo Indians, portions of these tribes being civilized, and others adhering to their wild and nomadic life in the mountains. They are one of the most

interesting features of the country. For
years savage members of the Yaqui tribe
have waged bloody and successful wars
against the Mexican Government, and
have been the principal cause of the slow
development of the Gulf coast ; but since
the death of their famous leader Cajeme
they have been peaceable and quiet. As
a race they are remarkably stalwart, hand-
some, and aggressive, and are said to be
able to endure any extremes of heat or
cold. They are enlisted in the service of
the government whenever it is possible,
and make the best soldiers obtainable for
this particular country.

While in Guaymas I heard from reli-
able sources that the *jabalí*, peccary, or
Mexican wild hog, was quite plentiful
along the line of the Sonora Railway,
and determined to get up a small party

and attack these pugnacious pigs in their own haunts. The *jabali* (pronounced hah-va-lee in the Mexican version of the Spanish language) is the wild hog of Northern Mexico, and while one of them is in no wise equal to the wild boar of other countries, still, as they go in droves, and are equal in courage, they more than make up in numbers all they lose by being considered individually. Up to this time my game list had included polar bears, chipmunks, moose, jack rabbits, grizzlies, snipe, elk, buffalo, snow birds, reindeer, vultures, panther, and others, but as yet the scalp of no peccary dangled from my belt. So one fine morning we pulled out for Torres station, about twenty or twenty-five miles up the railway, where peccaries could be expected, and where horses (better speaking, the bucking broncho of the Southwest) could be procured, together with guides, ropers-in, etc.

The fertile soil and warm sunshine of Sonora quickens the imagination in a way unknown in the northern part of the United States, with its colder clime and cloudy skies. The day before starting I had done a good deal of telegraphing up the Sonora railway to learn just where these peccaries might be the most numerous, and the replies were enthusiastic as well as comical. Carbo sent back word that the section men on the railway had to "shoo" the *jabalis* off the track so as to repair it ; another station reported that wild hogs were seen every day except Sundays ; another station said there was a Yaqui Indian guide there who went out with a lasso and a long, sharpened stick, and brought in a peccary every morning before breakfast ; while Torres thought I could have *jabali* about three miles from there. This was the most modest report and the nearest station, so I decided on Torres.

The country along the southern portion of the Sonora railway would be interesting in the extreme to one unfamiliar with tropical or sub-tropical countries. Its vegetation was most curious, and the surrounding country picturesque. Fine scenery can, indeed, be viewed in a thousand places in our own country, but it is not characterized with such a wonderful plant growth as we saw that morning on our way to the slaughter grounds of the peccaries. Here was the universal mesquite, looking like a dwarfed apple tree, and that affords the brightest fire of any wood ever burned. The tender of our engine was filled with it, and, as far as fuel was concerned, we could have made sixty miles an hour, had we wished to do so. The wood of the mesquite is of a beautiful bright cherry red ; many a time I have wondered if this plentiful, tough, and twisted timber of the far Southwest could not be utilized in some way as a fancy wood ; certainly a more beautiful color was never seen. Occasionally I thought I saw my old friend the sagebrush ; then there was the ironwood (*palo de hierro*), that looks like a very fine variety of the mesquite. Its name is derived from its hardness, and is well deserved. It requires an ax to fell each tree, and as the quality of different trees is always the same, and that of different axes is not, even this ratio of one ax to one tree has to be changed occasionally, and always in favor of the tree.   There was a story going the rounds that a tramp, who had wandered into that country (tramps sometimes get lost and find themselves in Sonora just once), with the usual appetite of his class applied for something to eat.   In reply he was told, if he would get out a certain number of rails for a fence, the proprietor would give him a week's board.   It was, as he thought, about a day's work that had been assigned him, and bright and early next morning he sallied out with his ax on his shoulder.   Unfortunately the most tempting tree he met was an iron-wood.   Very late in the evening he returned with the ax helve on his arm. " How many rails did you split to-day?" was asked.   "I did not split any, but

I hewed out one," was the reply ; and then he resigned his position.

There is also the *palo verde*, named for its color, with its bright, vivid green leaf, twig, and bark, and its pretty yellow blossoms, making a beautiful contrast with the more somber green of other trees. Occasionally great rows of cottonwoods (the *alamo* of the Mexicans) show the line of water courses, while a number of shrubs covered with blossoms are seen, apparently half tree, half cactus, so thick are their brambles and thorns. But as to cactus ! There are five hundred species in America, of which Mexico has a large plurality, and the majority of these can be found along this end of the Sonora railway. There is the giant pitahaya, sometimes with a dozen arms, each as big as an ordinary tree, and from thirty to forty feet in height. Each arm has a score of pulpy ribs along its sides, and each rib has a button of thorns every inch along its length, each button having twenty or twenty-four great thorns sticking from it. I was told that when a hunter is sorely pressed by peccaries, if he will climb a pitahaya about ten feet, the thorns are so thick and terrible in their effect that the peccaries will not dare to follow him, hardy and venturesome as they are. Then there is the choya or cholla cactus, about as high as one's waist. You can go around a pitahaya as you would a tree, but when you find a field of chopalla (field of choyas) you might as well try to go around the atmosphere to get to a given point. The cholla will lean over until it breaks its back trying to get in your way, so that

A PITAHAYA CACTUS.

it can dart a dozen or two spines into your flesh. They are the worst of all; I could use almost as much of my readers' time in describing different cactuses as I used of my own in picking them out of my flesh after the peccary hunt was over, but I forbear.

When we reached Torres nobody seemed to know anything about peccaries, and as the train stopped there for dinner we had plenty of time to talk it over. It then appeared that wild hogs were to be found all the way from Guaymas to Nogalles, but at this time of the year were very scarce, and seen only in twos or threes, and not in droves. In droves they are pugnacious and will easily bay; but in pairs or very small numbers they are more timid, and not until they are exhausted or overtaken by a swifter pursuer will they show fight. No *jabalis* could be depended on, and, as I had only a day or two to spare, I determined to move on to Carbo, where the prospects seemed better, and which place we reached in time for supper. This over we busied ourselves about our horses, mules, guides, dogs, etc. The superintendent of the railway at Guaymas had kindly volunteered to telegraph to any point and secure us a Yaqui Indian or two to guide us after the *jabalis*, and any number of hundreds of dogs to bay them if needed. He said he could guarantee the dogs (and so could any-one else who knew anything about a Mexican village), but he felt dubious about the Yaqui Indians. We secured four broncho horses and two dejected mules for the next day, and then went to

sleep. I unrolled my blankets and
buffalo robe, laid them down on the railway station platform, and, as the night
was cold, had a fine sleep. The morning broke as clear as crystal, and we were
up bright and early ; but in spite of all our
Caucasian hurry we did not get away until
shortly after nine o'clock. Our first destination was a ranch two miles to the south-
east of the town, owned by Colonel Muñoz.
Here we were to get a Yaqui Indian for
a guide, and learn the latest quotations
as to the peccary market. Shortly after
rising in the morning heavy clouds were
seen in the northeast, which kept spreading and coming nearer and nearer, with
vivid flashes of lightning and loud rum-
blings of thunder, until just about the
time we were halfway to the ranch of
Colonel Muñoz it broke over us with the

full fury of a Sonora thunderstorm. Its worst feature was its persistency. I never saw a thunderstorm hang on for six or seven hours before in all my life, but this did, much to our personal dis- comfort, and, worst of all, to the serious detriment of the hunt.

Arriving at the ranch, we found that the Yaqui Indian guide, who, by the way, was a famous peccary hunter, was absent, working on a distant part of the hacienda. Now a hacienda or ranch in Sonora is about as large as a county in most of our States, and it requires efficient messenger service to get over one inside of half a day. We sent for him, however, and as a small boy present volunteered the infor- mation that he thought he could guide the party to where a pig might be lurk- ing in the brush, we concluded we would

take a short spin with him while waiting
for the Yaqui Indian. He based his
expectation of a *jabali* on the rain that
had been falling, which sent the wild hogs

A MEXICAN JABALI.

out, made it easy to trail them, and
brought them to bay sooner than if the
weather had been dry. There was no
horse for the youngster to ride, so he was
taken on behind one of the party, and we
started out in the pelting rain after "the
poor little pigs," as one of the señoras of

the hacienda put it. As the poor little pigs have been known to keep a man up a tree for three days, we felt more like wasting ammunition than sympathy on them.

The rain now came down in torrents, vivid sheets of lightning played in our faces, and the rumbling of the thunder was often so loud we could not hear the shoutings of one another. Now, indeed, we were anxious to get a peccary ; for while a little rain helps the hunter in his chase after wild hogs, such a deluge is entirely against him. The dry gullies were running water that would swim a peccary, and this was in their favor in escaping from the dogs, for I should have said we had two dogs with us : one a noble-looking fellow for a hunt, and resembling a Cuban bloodhound, the other a most dejected-looking whelp, a cross between a mongrel and a cur. The whole affair was the sloppiest, wettest failure, and about noon we got back to the hacienda, looking like drowned rats. A good Mexican dinner of chili con carne, red peppers, tabasco, and a few other warm condiments was never better appreciated, and as the Yaqui Indian had put in an appearance we crawled back into our wet saddles, with our clothes sticking to us like postage stamps, and once more sallied out. While we were eating dinner the rain had ceased, and our otherwise dampened hopes had gone up in consequence; but when we were about a mile away it seemed as if the very floodgates of heaven had opened and let all the water down the back of our necks. Gullies we had crossed in coming out almost dry now ran noisy, muddy waters up to the horses' middle, and in some places halfway up their sides. Thus we kept along for an hour or so, wet to the skin, and even under the skin, cholla cactus burs sticking to us until we looked like sheep. About two o'clock we heard loud shouts, and away we tore through cactus spines and shrubby thorns, for it was a sign there were peccaries ahead. Indeed they were ahead, and we chased them for eight miles. The ground was slippery, and the unshod ponies went sliding around over it like cats on ice with clam shells tied to their feet. I weighed 265 pounds, and my small pony not over two or three times as much, and how he kept up with the others, swinging through choyallas and around thick mesquite brush is yet a mystery.

Occasionally a horse would get a bunch
of cactus in his fetlock joint, and then he
would turn up his heels to let the light-

CHASING THE JABALIS IN THE RAIN.

ning pick it out, regardless of his rider.
Once or twice the peccaries were sighted
as two faint gray streaks, just outlined
against the dark green brush, into which
they disappeared at once. Several times
it looked as if we ought to overtake them
in a minue or two, but that minute never
came. Our Yaqui guide was valiantly to
the front, making leaps over cactuses that

would have shamed a kangaroo, and keeping well ahead of the horses. Suddenly he stopped and gave up the chase on the near side of a broad river, the result of the rain. His face was melancholy in the extreme, and it was known he would not give up the chase without the best of reasons, as he was to receive a month's wages (five dollars) if a *jabali* were killed. He explained in Spanish that the party had been following the hogs with an absolute certainty of catching them, so tired had they become, when, to his dismay, the tracks of three other fresh peccaries were seen coming in at this point. Whenever fresh *jabalis* join those worn out enough to come to bay, the latter change their minds as to fighting, and will run as long as their fresh companions hold out. We thus would have

had another eight to twelve miles' chase
through the slippery mud, which the
horses and mules could not have endured,
so exhausted were they already. We had
seen the beasts, nevertheless, and in losing them had learned one of their distinct peculiarities, which fact was sufficient compensation for our first, but
never to be forgotten, hunt for wild
pigs.

The peccary, as already stated, is a
ferocious little beast, never hesitating,
when in numbers, to attack other animals.
The coyote leaves them alone if numerous, and even the mountain lion passes
them to look for other game. Their
tusks are deadly weapons, and they click
like so many hammers when the creature
is angry. If any ambitious Nimrod wants
a hunt after the most peculiar game extant

in the United States and Mexico he ought to take a peccary chase in Central Sonora.

The country around Guaymas is extremely fertile, and in no part of the American continent is there a richer country than lies along the eastern and northern portion of the Gulf of California. Sonora and Sinaloa are conceded to be the richest States in Mexico, and just as Mexico has been the most backward country of North America, so these two States are the least advanced portion of Mexico. This condition of affairs is due almost wholly to the same cause that has retarded the growth of Arizona and New Mexico, namely, the raids of hostile Indian tribes. These two States have not only been a favorite hunting and scalping ground for the

Apaches, but within their own borders
have been superior and warlike races to
contend with in the Yaqui and Mayo
Indians. The last war of the Yaquis
with the Mexican Government lasted over
twelve years, but since its close a number of years ago the Indians are settling
in the towns and villages, where they are
the most industrious portion of the working population. With the disappearance
of this disturbing element the most important problem regarding the growth
and development of the garden of the
Pacific appears to have been solved.
Every grade of climate can be found
here, from the tropical seacoast to the
temperate great plateaus, a short distance
inland. The country has a rich, well-
watered soil ; there are vast, well-wooded
mountain ranges, where all kinds of game

are found in abundance ; the rivers and bays are filled with every variety of fish, and two or more crops of fruits or staple articles can be raised yearly. Such a country cannot long remain unnoticed and unsettled; for when railways are constructed through it the attention of outsiders must be drawn to the land.

# CHAPTER IV.

CENTRAL CHIHUAHUA—FROM THE CITY OF
CHIHUAHUA WESTWARD TO THE GREAT
MEXICAN MINING BELT.

WHILE in Guaymas and discussing a practicable route into the heart of the Sierra Madres, I was told by the general commanding the division in which Guaymas was situated, and strongly advised by others having a knowledge of the country, not to attempt an entrance into the mountains from the western side, but rather from the high plateaus, of which the city of Chihuahua was the central point. There were many excellent reasons given for this advice. The Yaqui Indians were said to be very restless at that time; the season of the year was unfavorable, because all large rivers, like the Yaqui, Fuerte, and Mayo, were at their height; again, there were no good points near the mountains for outfitting such as the city of Chihuahua afforded. All these reasons, together with the advance of exceedingly warm weather, made me conclude to retrace my steps to the eastern side of the Sierra Madre range. So we again passed over the Sonora railway, and enjoyed those charming contrasts of the sea of flower-covered plains and mountains during the two days' ride that took us to Benson. Thence we returned to Deming, and from that point to El Paso, whence the Mexican Central Railway takes one in a night's ride about two hundred and fifty miles southward, to the city of Chihuahua.

This is a place of about thirty thousand people, and is the most important city in Northern Mexico. Like all towns in Mexico, but little of it can be seen from the railway, only the tall spires of its famous cathedral being visible ; but the fine church alone well repays the tourist for stopping over on his southern flight. Beside the cathedral, there are many other features of interest to the tourist having sufficient leisure, and the town should not be so universally slighted as it now is. It is the outfitting point for all parties visiting the many large and famous mines of the northern portion of the Sierra Madre range. The journey from the city to the mines is made by diligence for the first hundred miles, to the low-lying foothills of the mountains, and then by mule-back for one hundred or one hundred and fifty miles, to the heart of the great range. As this was nearly the route we wished to pursue, the first two days were passed in outfitting and making necessary arrangements. When we were informed that the diligence left Chihuahua at three o'clock in the morning, we were convinced that the Mexicans were by no means as indolent as they have been reported, especially in the matter of early rising, or they would not start out a stage at such an early hour. The conveyance must of necessity be seldom patronized by any persons except the natives; and the calling of passengers at that time for a seventy-five or eighty mile drive could only be accounted for by a morbid desire of the people to be up before the early bird. The day before leaving was passed in assorting all the baggage absolutely needed for a long trip by mule-back, and in getting together such necessary provisions as we would use.

I had been told that but little could be purchased after leaving the town, and then only at three or four times the expense of buying and transporting the same from Chihuahua. So despite all our efforts to cut down our luggage it had quite a formidable appearance, and I judged that my pack train would be an imposing affair, even if the daily bill of fare was not. Our traps were piled up in the office of the diligence, and orders were given to call us quite early, that we might be promptly on hand, for we were assured the diligence would wait for no man. Quite reluctantly I retired early, and left the pleasant crowd sitting on the piazza that surrounded the inner court of the hotel.   As the noises of one of these primitive Mexican hotels cease about one o'clock in the morning, and begin about two, and as the night watchman felt it incumbent to open my door every tour he made, and hold his lantern in my face to see whether I was having a good night's rest, there was little cause for alarm lest I should be left.   Nevertheless to make assurance trebly sure I was called by three different persons.   It was evidently a great event to have passengers leave by the diligence.   We were soon out in the streets, picking our way along in total darkness, trying to make the requisite number of twists and turns down the little side streets to the office (for this Mexican diligence was a proud affair, and would not stoop to drive to the hotel for passengers, not even for extra money). The rigid rules of the corporation had to be enforced, and were above all price ; so we went floundering around in utter darkness until we were waylaid by a friendly policeman with a lantern, who doubled us back on our tracks, and assisted us to reach the dark door of the diligence office, which, at that hour, was not distinguishable from any other door. At first we were sure the policeman had made a mistake, for there was no sign of life about the place, and it was full time for departure.

Soon, however, a frowzy-headed man with a candle in his hand opened the door and bade us enter ; but I preferred walking up and down outside in the cool morning air, and had a good half hour's exercise of that kind before the coach came lumbering into sight. The huge, old-fashioned affair had the queerest look imaginable ; for, hitched to it in groups of four each, with two leaders, were the tiniest mules I had ever seen. With the arrival of the coach and ten the office at once burst into life. I stood and counted my luggage as piece after piece was thrown on behind, and felt as though I was monopolizing the highway, for my freight towered up and filled the boot. The office was then examined to see that nothing had been left ; but, alas ! that precaution was a failure, as I found to my vexation at the end of the first day's drive. It was broad daylight when we finally got away at half-past five in the morning. Walking about in the cool air had given us voracious appetites, and

as we clattered by the humble huts of
the peons and saw them making their
simple morning meals, we regretted
exceedingly having placed any faith in
the punctuality of this particular diligence.
As we drove onward through the broad
avenue of *alamos* on the outskirts of the
town the fields were filled with the early
workmen, who rise as soon as it is light
for their work, and rest in the heat of
noonday. In this part of the country
these laborers are always dressed in
white that looks immaculate in the distance, against the dark background of the
fields, but it will not bear close inspection. I was thus able to prove another
virtue of the Mexican people, or at least
a certain portion of them, and this too
despite the fact that my discovery does
not accord with the generally accepted

American opinion of Mexican laborers. There was no doubt that they were unusually early risers to their work, as all that morning I found evidence of this fact. We drove twenty miles before breakfast, and passed people going into the city who had come as great a distance. As I have said, these same people take their siesta in the afternoon, and are judged accordingly by others who do not get up early enough to know what they have done.

Leaving Chihuahua and bearing west toward the Sierra Madres, one finds the road even crowded with Mexican transportation, all from the rich silver belt now being rapidly developed, chiefly by American wealth. There are great carts with solid wooden wheels of the Nazarene style, the patient donkey of the same period, and all so numerous that one would think there was an exodus from a city soon to be put under siege. Almost anything that grows about the home of a Mexican of the lower order furnishes an excuse for him to take it into town with a hope of selling it. Until we were fairly out of the suburbs our party were the only occupants of the coach, but there we were joined by a Mexican gentleman, the son of a wealthy mine owner, who lived back in the mountains. He was on his way to his father's mining district, and, as I had met him and talked with him before leaving, I had so timed my departure as to be with him for at least a part of the journey. The country directly back of Chihuahua reminded me greatly of our own plains by the imperceptible manner in which it rises toward the foothills of the mountains, although it was far more fertile and well watered, as the numbers of rich ranches along the way testified. At nine o'clock we stopped to eat breakfast and change mules. Our morning meal consisted of a concoction dignified by the name of coffee, with tortillas (the people's bread—pancakes of coarsely ground corn and water) and some stale eggs served in battered tin dishes upon a rough wooden box. The stage station being the only house in that part of the country, we could not be choosers. I noticed, however, that the soil was of the richest kind and well watered, so that anything could have been raised. What a paradise could be made by energy and industry where nature has already done so much.

At noon we stopped at one of the numerous simple and dreary little villages with which the country is studded. They appear far more desolate than the open, bare *mesa* lands. All are much alike, each having one or two streets of adobe houses, and a church of forbidding aspect, which fronts on a still more uninviting looking plaza, about fifty or seventy-five feet square, and set with whitewashed adobe benches, a stripe of green about the latter being almost the only thing to remind one of the color of verdure. The plaza is the pleasure ground of the people, and a more cheerless-looking place one could not imagine.

In investigating some of the resources of this country I ran across a (to me) new and interesting way of measuring wheat, and other products of the soil. I found

an old hunter on the Yukon River of
Alaska who measured the length of
grizzly bears by the fathom; I have had
a Mexican charge me for a saddle by the
pound, carefully weighing it and esti-
mating the resulting cost; and when I
tried to find how much an exceptionally
fine field of wheat yielded to the acre, the
reply was equally surprising. The owner,
as he boasted of the field, knew nothing
of so many bushels to the acre (or to the
hectare, which is their usual standard of
measurement), nor even of any ratio of
pounds or kilograms to a known area;
but he loudly bragged that he raised one
hundred for one, while only a few of his
neighbors could claim as high as fifty for
one, forty for one being the average for the
whole valley. Now one hundred for one
meant that he got one hundred grains for

every grain he planted, one hundred bushels for every bushel put in as seed. If he
had planted a bushel on an acre of ground
and got one hundred bushels in return it
would be considered an enormous yield,
and even a Western farmer would dance
with delight at such a result ; but if he
had planted a bushel on ten acres of
ground, and got the same hundred bushels as before, the Mexican farmer would
be as happy as ever, while the American
farmer would begin to wonder if the old
farm could stand a third mortgage or
not.

Of course the American will say that
about a certain number of bushels are
sown to the acre, and that one hundred
for one or fifty for one really gives us a
fair ratio in judging of the fertility of the
land. But I would answer that in Mexico

little attention is paid even to *such* a ratio, or to any other in agriculture, and only the most careful observation or inquiry can elicit the facts necessary for a basis of proper conjecture.

A Mexican diligence is ornamented with an assistant to the driver in the shape of a nimble young fellow, whose business it is to throw stones at the mules. He occupies the front seat alongside the driver, and whenever the mules have the appearance of commencing to walk— which occurs about every half minute— he jumps nimbly to the ground, makes a dash ahead for the leaders, with his hands and pockets full of stones, and pelts the unfortunate beasts well. Of course they make a tremendous burst of speed, and he grasps the straps on the side of the coach and swings himself on top; then the leaders look around, and, seeing him up out of the way, they slacken down their pace again, when the performance is repeated. Sometimes the mules do not wait to be pelted, but when they see their enemy stoop down to gather the missiles they gallop wildly ahead, leaving the road runner to make the best time he can to catch up ; which having done, he takes his revenge on the mules from above at his leisure.

If there is one thing in which the Mexicans can outdo us more than another it is in stage or diligence driving, and this too with animals that will not compare with ours in size or strength, although, in proportion to their size, probably more enduring. They generally make up in numbers what they lack in strength, for they hitch them in troops and droves, so to speak. When we first started we had two groups of four and two leaders; then we changed to four abreast and two wheelers; then, as the country grew a little rougher, they hitched two leaders to the six, making eight altogether. Now, again, we dropped to six mules in pairs, as we see them at home. As the last stretch was a tough one, we again had ten mules in sets of fours with two wheelers. This over a very rough mountain road. Here was versatility in mule driving that I never expected to see among a people that are generally reported by most American writers to be of a decidedly non-versatile character.

When the Mexican mules are through staging they "skirmish" for a living, grazing off such grass as can be had, or in lieu thereof browsing on cottonwood

and willow bush, not even disdaining a
corner of a corral or a wagon tongue or
two if times are going a little hard with
them. Late in the afternoon we realized
that we were entering the foothills of the
mountains, for the road wound through
many picturesque little ravines and
ascended the rocky beds of the small
creeks, often taking to the middle of the
stream when the cañon was very narrow
or thickly strewn with bowlders. It was
quite a common occurrence for the stage
to be overturned on the road—if road
it could be called—and the most decided
talent in mule driving was necessary to
guide the groups of little animals safely
between the mossy rocks. Toward evening the walls of the long cañon, with its
broken craigs and fantastic turrets, almost
met overhead, so narrow was it; but

after a few turns and twists it widened, and after rounding the peak of a high mountain, entered another cañon, where, strung out its whole length, was the town of Cusihuiriachic. I do not intend to throw the name of this Mexican town at my readers without giving a plan, section, and elevation of it as a key to the riddle. We were now in the land of the Tarahumari Indians of West Central Chihuahua, this long-winded name applying to them just as equivalent Indian names are found in Maine and a few other places in the Union. This large Indian tribe, probably numbering from 15,000 to 18,000 (the most authentic estimate I can get places them at 16,000, although I have heard them estimated at 30,000 in strength), was once scattered over a considerable territory, and their

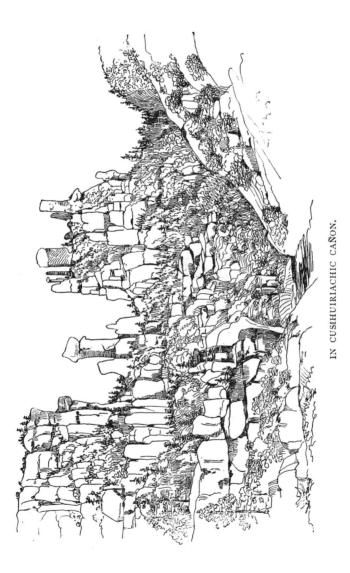

IN CUSIHUIRIACHIC CAÑON.

names are still given to most of the places in the country they occupied before the advent of Europeans.

Wherever there is water (so I was told by an old resident among these strange and little known people, Don Enrique Muller) the name of the camp or town alongside ended in *chic*, as in the example I have given above, as also in Bibichic, Carichic, Baquiriachic, and a few others I could mention—"all wool and a yard wide." The rest of the word Cusihuiriachic, still long enough for five or six more names, means, says my authority, "the place of the standing post." When they ruled their own country many years ago the principal means of punishment employed was the upright post, to which the offenders were tied and treated to a Delaware dissertation. Such

is the origin of the big name of the little
Mexican town of Cusihuiriachic, situated
about halfway between the city of Chihuahua and the great mining belt of the
Sierra Madres, west and southwest of the
city, and to which it is a secondary dis-
tributing point.   The diligence ride is
made to it in one day, a little over seventy-
five miles.   The place claims five thousand
people, and there is but one street up the
narrow gulch, which, however, is long
enough to justify its name.   It is wholly a
mining town, and has some important
quartz mills strung out along the little
stream through its principal and only
street.   When we reached our destination
for the night we found a square adobe
inclosure, with an enormous gateway,
through which the stage rattled and then
stopped in a small court for us to dis-

mount. From there we passed through another large gate into a similar court, filled with a variegated assortment of mules, and after dodging among them, to cross to the opposite side, we climbed three or four steps, and entered the most primitive hotel any civilized man's eyes ever rested on.

The patio or interior plaza of the hotel was, upon our arrival, being used as a cockpit, and one or two hundred people were jammed therein. Beside the Mexicans, there was one immense, brawny Chinaman. In the middle of the pit lay two dead cocks; one belonged to the Chinaman, and the other to some member of the Mexican aristocracy of the town. An adverse decision had just been given regarding the victory of the Chinaman's cock, and he was in the act of rolling up his sleeves to pitch into the crowd and vindicate the prowess of his fowl; fortunately our timely arrival prevented any further strife by diverting attention to us, while the host was dragged from the midst of the fray to hunt up a key to unlock one of the narrow pens—called rooms— that overlooked the mule corral. Here, on a dirty brick floor, my bedding was spread, and I slept to a chorus of squealing mules, which came in through the grated, wooden-shuttered window. And right here I may say that I know of no better opening for Americans of small means than starting and keeping hotels in Mexican towns, where decent accommodations of the kind are wanting, and where a great many Americans, as well as English and other foreigners, pass through. I could mention fifty such towns beside the example given. In the town referred to we were crowded, four and six together, into those small pens— all travelers passing backward and forward on business connected with mining interests or similar industries. It seemed to be the universal custom of this portion of the country to get up at three o'clock to take the diligence, no matter how long or short the drive was to be. We were going only forty miles farther the next day to Carichic ; the diligence returned nearly eighty miles to Chihuahua, and another stage line branched off for Guerrero, to the northwest ; but it appeared necessary that passengers should rise at the same hour in order that all the coaches might get away at the same time.

The Carichic line is quite unfrequented, and only an ordinary wagon is used as a stage for the few Mexicans who go that way; but in honor of my party the large diligence was sent that day to carry us and all our luggage. With the first streak of dawn we were threading our way backward and forward across the little stream that runs through the town, past sleeping pigs, geese, chickens, dogs, burros, and Mexicans— an almost indiscriminate mass strung along the roadside. This road led past the big quartz mill, grinding away day and night, and by it we climbed up and out of the narrow cañon till the *mesa* and the hills were reached. Afterward the drive was through beautiful park-like places, with groves of oak and pine, the road winding up and down the mountain side, until, early in the afternoon, we reached Carichic. On the road between

Cusihuiriachic and Carichic we came to an adobe building, that departed in a very picturesque way from the everlasting

MEXICAN ADOBE HOUSE FORTIFIED AGAINST APACHE RAIDS.

mud box style of architecture so common to this country, and for which departure we had to thank the Apaches. Not that they built it, for an Apache never built anything except under compulsion, and at that time compulsion of these Indians was about the scarcest thing in Mexico; but, rather, they compelled the Mexicans to do it, that is, to erect corner towers at the four corners of the mud box, and convert it into a building of defense.  In the picturesque mountain scenery it looked at a short distance away like an old castle, and only a nearer inspection dispelled the illusion.

While at Cusihuiriachic we had looked with some contempt on the primitive accommodations of its forlorn and dilapidated hotel, and had rather scouted the idea of its being possible to find a worse place or greater disregard for the common necessities of life in any habitable town.  The little cell-like room, with its wooden bench, tin wash basin, and bare brick floor on which to stow one's bedding, seemed to be the extreme of simplicity; therefore we believed that Carichic could hardly do less for us. But as everything is relative in this world, I was soon to look back to the despised hotel as the last taste of civilization, and to appreciate it accordingly. On reaching Carichic, a town of six or seven hundred people, we were told there was no such thing as a lodging house for us, and that it would be necessary for us to camp in the streets or some field, unless our Mexican friend could induce the village priest to allow us the use of a large empty room in one corner of the big building he occupied. The loaning or renting of a large empty room does not seem to be an act of great hospitality, nevertheless it was so regarded. The Mexican gentleman, when passing backward and forward over the trail between his father's mines and Chihuahua, always made his headquarters with the priest or

*cura*, who was a great friend of his family ;
but everything and everybody from the
United States he looked upon with sus-
picion and distrust.    Therefore, consider-
ing the circumstances, his readiness to
allow us under his roof could only be
considered as a marked hospitality, or as
evidence of a disposition to oblige our
mutual Mexican friend.    Perhaps he was
animated by a keen sense of duty, and
found this a fitting opportunity to mortify
the spirit.    But, whatever his motive, we
were given the use of the room.    So the
stage left us and our worldly possessions
there, for at Carichic all roads ended, and,
as soon as I could make my arrangements
with a native packer for his pack train of
mules, we were to take one of the narrow
Indian trails leading back into the heart
of the Sierra Madres.

The priest's house was by far the most important in the village, being built around a large interior court, with all the rooms facing on this court, except the one given for our use. At the entrance to this interior court was a large gate, which could be barricaded in case of danger or an Indian uprising. On one of the outside corners of the structure was a sort of storeroom, the door opening on the street, and next to this store-room—which contained a few old bottles and pieces of leather — was the room assigned to us. At one end of our room was a small fireplace, and along the rude adobe wall was a wooden bench, and near it a table. One window, with wooden bars, and the door, were the only openings. The floor was the common one of earth. As there was not a place in the town where food could be bought, it was necessary to open our boxes before our dinner could be prepared. Wood and water were soon brought, a fire started in the fireplace, and our simple meal could have been ready in fifteen minutes —and would have been anywhere except under the auspices of our Mexican cook. We tried to secure chickens and eggs— staple articles even on the frontier of Mexico—but were told that time would be required to get them, and that the next day would be the earliest moment at which they could be procured. Tortillas, however, were forthcoming, and these, with bacon, hard bread, cheese, and tea, made an excellent meal. Dionisio, or Dionysius in English, my cook, had been highly recommended to me at Chihuahua, and had been brought with me on that account, as I had been influenced by glowing descriptions of his supposed good qualities. Since the morning of our start from Chihuahua he had been the butt and laughingstock of even the slowest of the Mexicans, who had heaped all sorts of derisive epithets on him for his general stupidity. My only hope was that he would blossom out as a good cook when he had an opportunity; but here I was doomed to receive the full shock of his utter incapacity, and to realize that he would only shine resplendently as a complete failure on the whole journey. Finally I was forced to the conclusion that he was palmed off on me simply to get him salaried and off the the hands of somebody else. Although we arrived at Carichic about noon, or shortly after, and preparations were begun at once for our simple meal, we were compelled to eat it by the light of a tallow candle. It was evident that, if more than one meal a day was to be had, Dionicio would require an assistant to do all the work.

As night approached the good padre tendered us the use of his parlor floor on which to spread our bedding. This room occupied one side of the interior court. It was a long, narrow place without windows, and lighted only through the wooden doorways, of which there were two. In one end of the room was a little old narrow iron bedstead; at the other a small, black haircloth sofa, and a couple of chairs. On the walls were a picture of the Virgin and a small crucifix, while in another part, hung up beyond reach of the tallest man, was a small,

a very small mirror, evidently regarded
as a profane thing and not to be used.
In the center of the room was a small
strip of faded green Brussels carpet.
The whole place had a most depressing
air, and the bare earthen room outside
was beautiful by comparison, for in the
latter we had the sunshine, and could see
the lovely blue sky, and all around the
horizon, the rolling, tree-covered hills,
with the distant peaks of the Sierra
Madres in the background. Nature had
been very lavish with this place, and at
every point of the compass it was picturesque and beautiful in the extreme.
About Carichic the soil is wonderfully
fertile and the grass luxuriant. A lovely
little mountain river winds by on one
side of the village. The people are
principally the civilized Tarahumari In-

dians, and this is one of their largest towns. There is, however, as in all Indian towns, a slight sprinkling of Mexicans, and to that portion of the community we looked for mules to carry us back into the mountains.

Shortly after my arrival a number of Indians were started out to look up the animals; for we wished to get away the next morning if possible. When night came a part of the needed complement had not been found; for Mexican mules are always turned loose to hunt their living, and they often wander off many miles, and it sometimes takes days to find them. All night long the Indians were again out scouring the hills, but in the morning there were still not mules enough; so nothing could be done but patiently await their arrival. The next morning Francisco, a most excellent packer, by taking one horse to carry a few light bundles, had animals enough to make a start. Horses are of no service whatever in these mountains. On the steep, rough, dangerous trails the small Mexican mule is the only animal that can possibly cling, crawl, and climb up and down the dizzy heights. The motley and scraggy assortment of beasts led up for our inspection that morning gave us the uncomfortable feeling that we would never reach any place if we trusted to them. A little before ten o'clock my train of fourteen mules was started ; and we were told we must ride fast, as the trail just out of the town was good, and it was necessary to make the noon camp at a certain spot. The trail we took was one seldom used, except by the

Indians, and a few Mexicans who held mining property in that portion of the mountains. It was, therefore, one of the roughest and steepest in that region. Instead of seeking any sort of grade, it struck out wherever fancy had dictated to the original Indian travelers, generally over the steepest peaks or along the edge of some high and dizzy precipice, even when this course was wholly unnecessary. Although that made it somewhat laborious for us, as well as our animals, it gave us unusually fine views and picturesque effects, and despite the roughness of the trail we rode fifteen miles that morning and made our noon camp on time.

When but a very short distance out of Carichic, while crossing a high ridge, I observed, in a little valley below, a curious looking creature skulking along half hidden from view, toward the entrance to a cave in a huge bowlder. I called the attention of my Mexican companion to him, and he said he was only one of the wilder Tarahumari Indians, who lived in this manner, and that I would see enough of them before I finished my journey. This was my first introduction to a strange people hidden away in those grand old mountains, and of which the world has known comparatively nothing.

# CHAPTER V.

CENTRAL CHIHUAHUA—IN THE LAND OF
THE LIVING CAVE AND CLIFF DWELLERS
—THE TARAHUMARI INDIANS, CIVILIZED
AND SAVAGE.

I PROPOSE to devote the greater portion of this chapter to a consideration
of the Tarahumari Indians of Central and
Southwestern Chihuahua, a tribe of aborigines that I have occasionally seen
mentioned in works and articles on Mex·
ico (especially its northern part), but of
which I can find no detailed account anywhere in the literature I possess of this
region. The fact of my having been in
that country for some time, seeing and

investigating some of their most curious habitations and customs, coupled with what information I could get from a few hardy Mexican pioneers in the fastnesses of the great Sierra Madre range, who corroborate each other, constitutes the basis of my comments.

Although the Tarahumari tribe of Indians are not at all well known—for I doubt if many of my readers have ever heard of them—they are, nevertheless, a very numerous people, and were they in the United States or Canada, where statistics of even the savages are much better kept than in Mexico, they would have an almost world-wide reputation. On account of this utter lack of statistics it is impossible to state with close approximation the number of Tarahumari Indians in this part of the country. So I will

have to rely on the estimates (really broad
guesses) of those best informed, giving
my readers the benefit of my own researches as a check, although not claim-
ing they will make a very good one, to
the wide range of estimates made by
others.   In a previous chapter I spoke of
the number of these Indians, but really
am inclined, from all I could learn of
them, to estimate their number at twenty
thousand or thereabouts.   An Indian
tribe of twenty thousand people in our
own country would be heard of often
enough in press and public to become a
household word ; but the isolation of the
Tarahumari Indians from the beaten lines
of travel, and the little interest taken in
them by local and governmental officials
(especially the interest which would make
their habitations, habits, and customs

known to the world) have thrown a veil
over them both dark and mysterious.
Some tribes of no greater strength in the
interior of Africa are better known to us
at home than are these Tarahumaris of
the Sierra Madre Mountains of Mexico.
They are now seldom seen in the city of
Chihuahua, or even on the diligence lines
radiating to the many western points
which draw their supplies from this
town ; and it is only when the mule trails
to the deeply hidden mountain mines are
taken that they are seen at all. Still
better, if one cuts loose from these too,
he will be yet more likely to find them in
all their rugged primitiveness. Those
usually seen by the white traveler to these
parts are called civilized, and live in log
huts, tilling a bit of mountain slope, not
unlike the lower classes of Mexico, whom

they copy in their departure from established habits.   It is no wonder, therefore,
that little has been said about them more

A CIVILIZED TARAHUMARI HOUSE.

than to mention occasionally where they
once lived in a country now held by a
higher civilization.

Even the word " Chihuahua " itself is a
Tarahumari word, and was applied to
the site of the present city of Chihuahua ;
its meaning is " the place where our best
wares were made."   The territory lying
between the line of the Mexican Central

Railway (which cuts through a small part of their ancient country) and the Sierra Madres proper, or where diligences cease to go and all transportation is done on mule-back or with donkeys, the Tarahumaris have abandoned to invading civilization, or have obeyed its mandates and become civilized themselves. They are only found in a primitive state in the Sierra Madres, with the far greater excess on the eastern slopes of the wide range. Beyond the Tarahumaris to the west are the Mayo and Yaqui tribes of Indians, on the rich and level slopes of the Mexican States of Sinaloa and Sonora; while on the north they come in contact with the omnipresent and widely feared Apache, whose hand was against everyone and everyone's hand against him.

Though a peaceful tribe of Indians, as

far as their relations with Mexico have been concerned, they nevertheless were not wanting in the elements that made them good defenders of their land ; and the Apaches, so dreaded by others, gave the mountainous country of the Tarahumaris a wide berth when on their raids in this direction. The Tarahumaris, equally armed, which they seldom were, were more than a match for these Bedouins of the boundary line between our own country and Mexico. One who had ever seen a group of the wild Tarahumaris would not credit them with a warlike or aggressive disposition, or even with much of the defensive combativeness that is necessary to fight for one's country. Even the semi-civilized among them are shy and bashful to a point of childishness that I have never seen elsewhere among Indi-

ans or other savages ; and I have lived
among nine-tenths of the Indian tribes of
the United States and a great number
outside of our domains. Heretofore the
Eskimo of North Hudson Bay I deemed
the most modest of savages, but they are
brigands compared with the Tarahumari
natives. If they have the least intimation
of a white man's approach, he stands as
little show of seeing them as if they were
some timid animal fleeing for life.

A Mexican gentleman who owns a part
interest in a rich silver mine in the great
broken Barrancas leading out from the
Sierra Madre toward the Pacific side, or
into the States of Sinaloa and Sonora
(but who always reached his mine by way
of Chihuahua), told me that he had several
times passed over the mountain trail on
mule-back, when with a pack train, and

not seen a single Tarahumari, although the trip occupied a number of days in their country, and took him where he should have seen two or three hundred if they had made no effort to escape his notice. The country thereabouts is well wooded and often heavily timbered, and the timid native, hearing the clang of the mule shoes on the rough, rocky trail, will at once retire to the seclusion of the nearest thick brush, and there wait until the intruder is out of sight.

They do not fly like a flock of quails suddenly surprised by the hunter, however, for, if caught, they generally stand and stare it out rather than seem to run from the white man while directly in his presence ; but if the latter is vigilant and keeps his eyes wide open, he will often see them skulking away among the trees

or behind the rocks as he is approaching
their houses, or the caves or cliff dwellings wherein they abide. Of course, as

AN INDIAN HOME BETWEEN ROCK PILLAR AND TREE.

one would naturally expect, the more
savage Tarahumari natives, or those
living in the rocks, cliffs, and caves, or
brush jacals, are much wilder and more
timid than those pretending to adopt the
forms and duties of civilization. It is

this peculiarity that has made it so hard
to understand or learn anything about
them, and this too in a land where so
little interest is taken in gaining knowledge of the subject.

In my wanderings through this portion
of the Sierra Madres (and right here I
might state that on some Mexican maps
this portion of the great range is occasionally labeled as the *Sierra de Tarahumari,*
about the only place we ran across the
name) I was more fortunate in seeing a
large number of them engaged in more
nearly all the labors and duties they are
known to follow than is usually the case:
the civilized Tarahumari, living in rough
stone and adobe houses, with brush
fences around his cultivated fields; and
the most savage of the race, acknowl-
edging none of the Mexican laws or

customs, and living in caves in the rocks or under the huge bowlders, or in cliffs high up the almost perpendicular faces of the rock, where they probably tend a few goats and plant their corn on steep slopes, using pointed sticks to make the holes in the ground into which the grains are deposited.

In appearance the Tarahumari savage is, I think, a little above the average height of our own Indians in the Southwest. They are well built, and very muscular, while the skin of the cave and cliff dweller is of the darkest hue of any American native I have ever seen, being almost a mixture of the Guinea negro with the average copper-colored aborigine that we are so accustomed to see in the western parts of the United States. The civilized Tarahumaris are generally no-

ticeably lighter in hue.  The Mayos and
Yaquis on the west, the Apaches to the
north, the Tepehuanes to the south, and
the Comanches to the east are lighter in
their complexions than the cave- and cliff-
dwelling Tarahumaris, although they live
in much warmer climates than the latter.
There is every opportunity to inspect the
skin of the savage Tarahumari, as they
wear only a breechclout and a pair of
rawhide sandals; and if it be a little
chilly—as it always is at evening, at
night time, and morning on the elevated
plateau land or mountainous regions of
Mexico—they may add a *serape* of mountain goat's wool over their naked shoulders.  Their faces generally wear a mild,
pleasing expression, and their women are
not bad-looking for savages, although the
older women break rapidly in appearance

after passing thirty to thirty-five years, as nearly as I could judge their ages. The savage branch of the Tarahumaris is of course the more interesting as the most nearly representing our own Indians of fifty to one hundred years ago, or before white men came among them. The civilized are not unlike those we have cultivating the soil in a rude way around the western agencies ; although those of Mexico have no governmental aid such as we so often and so lavishly pour into the laps of our copper-colored brethren of the North.

The savage Tarahumari lives generally off all lines of communication, shunning even the mountain mule trails if he can. His abode is a cave in the mountain side or under the curving interior of some huge bowlder on the ground.

The Sierra Madre Mountains, where they live, are extremely picturesque in their rock formation, giving thousands of shapes I have never see elsewhere— battlements, towers, turrets, bastions, buttresses and flying buttresses, great arches and architraves, while everything from a camel to a saddle can be descried in the many projecting forms.   It is natural that in such formation—a curious blending of limestone pierced by more recent up- heavals of eruptive rock—many caves should be found, and also that the huge, irregular, granitic and gneissoid bowlders, left on the ground by the dissolving away of the softer limestone, should often lie so that their concavities could be taken advantage of by these earth-burrowing savages.

The first cliff dwellers I saw were on

the Bacochic River, the first day out on mule-back from Carichic. These cliff dwellers had taken a huge cave in the limestone rock, some seventy-five feet above the water and almost overhanging the picturesque stream. They had walled up its outward face nearly to the top, leaving the latter for ventilation probably, as rain could not beat in over the crest of the butting cliff. It had but one door, closed by an old torn goat hide, through which the inhabitants had to crawl, like the Eskimo into their snow huts or *igloos*, rather than any other form of entrance I can liken it to. The only person we saw was a "wild man of the woods," who, with a bow and arrows in his hand and the skin of a wild animal around his loins for a breechclout, was skulking along the big bowlders near the foot of the cliff. A dozen determined men inside this cliff dwelling ought to have kept away an army corps not furnished with artillery, although I doubt if the occupants hold these caves on account of their defensive qualities, but rather for their convenience as places of habitation, needing but little work to make them subserve their rude and simple wants. My Mexican guide said they would only fly if we visited them, leaving a little parched corn, a rough *metate* or stone for grinding it, an unburned *olla* to hold their water, and some skins, and, perchance, worn-out native blankets for bedding; so I desisted from such a useless trip as getting over to their eyrie to inspect it.

About three months before my first expedition into Mexico, I saw a notice going the rounds of the press that living

cliff dwellers had been seen in the San
Mateo Mountains of New Mexico, and
that as soon as the snow melted a
mounted party would be organized to
pursue and capture them ; but I have
heard nothing from it, beyond the little
stir created at the time, and which the
finding of any living cliff dwellers anywhere would be likely to create. Yet
here are people of that description, of
whom the world seems to have heard
nothing. How many there are of them,
as I have already said, it seems hard to
tell. We saw at least five to six hundred
scattered around in the fastnesses of this
grand old mountain chain, and could
probably have trebled this if we had been
looking for cave and cliff dwellers alone
along and off our line of travel. Let us
place them at only three thousand in

strength, and we would have enough to write a huge book upon, giving as start-ling developments as one could probably make from the interior of some wholly unknown continent—in fact more curi-ous ; for the public is somewhat prepared for such a story by the large number of old deserted cliff dwellings found in Ari-zona and New Mexico, which have often been assigned to a people older than the ruins of the Toltec or Aztec races.   That there is some relation between these old cliff dwellers and the new ones I think more than likely ; and I believe that most writers who have seen both, or rather the ruins of the former and much of the life of the latter, as I have, would agree with me in this view.

It is pretty clearly settled that the Apaches are Athabascans, and came from

the far north ; and it seems not unlikely
that they drove southward or extermi-
nated the northern cliff dwellers, leaving
only these here as representatives, although numerous beyond belief, of a most
curious race generally supposed to be extinct.  The Pueblo Indians, of the same
locality, by living in larger communities
and stronger abodes were better able to
resist these Indian Northmen, and consequently some of their towns still exist ;
but the old cliff dwellers, like the new
ones, could in many cases be cut off from
water by a persistent and aggressive
enemy, such as the Apaches must have
been then, when just fresh from their
northern excursion.  It is still more probable, however, that they drove them
southward until the retreating cliff dwellers became so powerful by being massed

upon their southern brothers that they could resist further aggression, and therefore give successful battle to their old foe, as we know they have been able to do recently when the Apaches were performing such destructive work in this part of the country.

It is a well-known fact in archæology that a badly defeated people, driven from their country by a superior force of numbers, and occupying a new and less desirable tract, will generally reproduce their habitations, implements of the chase, and all other things which they may be called upon to construct in a much less perfect manner than when in their own country; and I found the cave and cliff dwellings of the wild Tarahumaris in the Sierra Madre Mountains to be in general less perfect than the cliff dwellings far to the

north, as those near Flagstaff, Ariz.,
the cave and cliff dwellings in the Mancos
Cañon, and many others I could mention in our own Southwest. Whatever
may be the relation between the dead
and departed northern cliff dwellers and
their southern living representatives, it
seems to me that it would well pay some
scientist to devote a few years to their
thorough study, as Catlin did so well
among the Sioux, Cushing with the
Zunis, and many others I could mention.

All these Tarahumaris, whether civilized to the extent of agriculture, living
in houses, and having the other arts in a
crude degree, and embracing Christi-
anity, or whether in the most savage
state, naked to the skin except rawhide
sandals, and living in caves or cliffs, while
still worshiping the sun, and hoping for

the return of Montezuma some day, all are to a great extent independent of the Mexican Government, much more than are any of the peaceable Indians of the United States from our own government, unless it be a few almost unknown tribes in the interior of Alaska. If a Tarahumari commits a crime against, or does an injury to, a Mexican or foreigner, the Mexican Government takes notice of it and tries to punish the offender; but between themselves, except in a few cases of flagrant murder, they can conduct all administration of justice, as well as other matters, wholly by officers of their own selection and by their own codes and customs. The very wild ones—the cliff and cave dwellers—know nothing of Mexican affairs, and in fact fly from all white people like so many quails when they approach. The more civilized elect their own chiefs and obey their executive mandates so well, as a general thing, that there is really very little reason for the Mexicans to force their officials upon them, if their only object is a maintenance of peace. Still the half-wild tribes of some parts of the mountains even war against each other without asking the Mexican Government yes or no, and conclude their own treaties as a result of such quarrels on their own basis. I was informed by Mr. Alberto Mendoza, a perfect master of both Spanish and English, and an interpreter at one of the big Sierra Madres silver mines, where there also was employed an excellent Tarahumari interpreter, that such a war as I have described recently broke out and was carried on by two factions in adjoining parts of the mountains. It was a very strange affair, of course, but I doubt if its existence was even known in any other part of Mexico.

Singularly enough, the badge of office of the self-governing tribes is a scepter, if an ornamented stick held in the hand can be called a scepter. These black savages of the sierras obey it more implicitly, however, than if it were a loaded Gatling gun trained on them. Whenever a government official or justice seizes this mace of the Madre Mountains, and holds it aloft, every person in sight is quelled more effectually than if it were a stick of giant powder that would explode if they did not obey. Its name among them, translated, is "God's Justice," and certainly no superstitious people ever obeyed a mandate more readily and com-

pletely than do they this mute expression
of their own laws, and without which
they would often be lawless under the
same circumstances.

An almost ludicrous case was told me
of a foul murder having been committed
by the wild Tarahumaris on the person
of a civilized one, the murderers holding
possession of the body. It was natural
that the civilized faction should want the
corpse for burial, and they demanded it,
but it was refused. The civilized natives
then went to the boundary line of the
two factions, hoping to get the chief of
the wild savages to assist them. Here
they found some four or five hundred of
the latter drawn up in battle array, with
bows and arrows, to dispute their passage
into their own land. The chief was
absent and refused to come to the assist-

ance of the others, although demanded in the name of the Mexican law, with corresponding punishment. The civilized natives then conceived the idea of a small body of picked men going in a roundabout way to compel his attendance, which was done, although he still refused to exercise his authority to compel his own band to give up the corpse of the dead Tarahumari. The forcing of the wild chief into the dispute was about to bring on a collision between the two factions, when one of the civilized natives wrenched his scepter from his hand, waved it aloft, and demanded of the wild ones that they cease all hostile demonstrations and bring in the body of the murdered man, all of which they did in the name of " God's Justice."

Nearly all the civilized Tarahumaris

are Christianized, while the wild ones
living in cliffs and caves are—if they can
be called anything—still worshipers of the
sun and believers in the return of Montezuma ; so this " God's Justice," as repre-
sented so effectually by the mace or scepter, cannot mean solely the Christian God
or that of the Tarahumaris, for in either
case it would have no effect on the other.
There can be only one conclusion that I
can see, and that is that this badge of
authority is as old as the Tarahumaris
themselves, or at least antedates the con-
version of the civilized ones by the old
Jesuits, or the conquering of the country
by the Spaniards from Europe. The
Mexicans use nothing of the kind except,
probably, in their state and federal legis-
latures, as we do in some of ours, and it
is not at all likely that these natives,

especially the wild ones, would have borrowed it from so distant and almost never
visited a source.

The civilized Tarahumaris have their
own elections, patterned after the Mexicans in a crude way, while the wilder
ones have their chiefs, but whether they
are elected or hereditary I was not able
to ascertain ; I am inclined to think it is
the former.

The wildest known of the Tarahumari
cliff and cave dwellers are probably those
of the Barranca del Cobre, which can be
seen from the Grand Barranca of the
Urique, as one skirts its dizzy cliffs, being
in fact a spur of the Grand Barranca leading out to the east.   There are undoubtedly many other, but unknown, places
where these savages dwell, if possible
more primitive than those of the Barranca

del Cobre. In this cañon the cliff dwellers
are often stark naked, except for a pair of
*guarraches*, or rawhide sandals, these
protecting the soles of the feet from the
flint-like broken rocks of this part of the
country, and without which even their
tough hides would soon be disabled.
Upon the approach of whites they fly to
their birdlike houses in the precipitous
cliffs like so many timid animals seeking
their burrows.

The next nearest grade of these people
goes so far as to ornament the person
with breechclouts after the latest fashion
set by Adam and Eve, the more savage
of these again using the skins of wild
animals for this purpose, while the better
grade manages to secure some dirty
clothes from the others to finish out this
necessary part of their wardrobe. When

it is reflected that the winters are quite severe on the higher parts of these sierras, the snow being some winters two and three feet deep, it is quite easy to conceive what constitutional toughness these fellows must have in their scanty attire.

An Eskimo would long to get back to the Arctic if he were here, so he could sit on an iceberg and get warm.

On the great mountain trails their feats of endurance are almost of a marvelous character. The semi-civilized are often employed as couriers, mail carriers, etc., and in all cases they invariably make from three to five times the distance covered by the whites in the same time, while there is no known domesticated animal that can possibly keep pace with them in the mountains.

It takes six or seven hours of fairly continuous climbing to make, by mule-back, from the mine in a deep gulch to the "cumbra," or crest of the Barranca del Cobre, by a most difficult mountain trail, the ascent made being five thousand to six thousand feet. It takes four hours to descend in the same way. A message was sent from "la cumbra" by a Tarahumari foot runner to a person at the mine and an answer received in an hour and twenty minutes, the same messenger carrying the letter both ways, or making the round trip.

One day a Tarahumari carrier passed us just after we had gone into camp about three o'clock in the afternoon, bound for the same point we expected to reach in three days' hard travel by mule-back. I wanted to send a message by him to this place, and on ascertaining when he would reach it was, as my hearers will easily infer, somewhat astonished to find out that he expected to make it that night, and I was afterward informed that he had done so.

Not a great many years ago the mail from Chihuahua to Batopilas was carried by a courier on his back, who made the distance over the Sierra Madre range, a good 250 miles, and return, or a total of 500 miles, in six days. Here he rested one day and repeated his trip, his contract being for weekly service. Alongside of this the best records ever made in the many six days' "go-as-you-please" contests that are heard of in the great cities of the United States sink into almost contemptible insignificance. I could give a dozen other instances, but

these are enough.   Of course these runners   make   many   " cut   offs "   from   the
established mule trails when their   course
is along  them,  and  they  thus  save  distance, but making all such allowance their
endurance is still phenomenal.

# CHAPTER VI.

THROUGH THE SIERRA MADRES—ON MULE-
BACK WESTWARD FROM CARICHIC.

AS our next month was passed on mule-back, and Mexican mule-back at that, I think it would be not at all inappropriate to make a brief dissertation on this kind of brute for the necessary merits and demerits of the journey.

The Mexican mule is a sort of a cross between a mountain goat and a flying squirrel, with the distinct difference that its surplus electricity flows off from the negative pole instead of the positive, as with the goat. It is in its meanderings on the mountain trail that it shines

resplendent, but with a luster wholly its
own, that can be no more compared with
any other than can the flash of the
diamond be compared with the fire of the
opal. I would like to place it alongside
of the American mule for comparison in
the "deadly double column" of the newspaper, but the Mexican beast would kick
out the intervening rule and "pi" the
type before enough was up to form an
opinion. On the mountain trail this distinct species of mule was never known to
fall, although he has an exasperating and
blood-curdling way of stumbling along
over it that would raise the hair of a bald-
headed man on end. Many a time I
have watched the mule I was compelled
to ride with a view of discovering his
methods of trying to frighten me to death
as payment for past injuries. Oftentimes

the trail would lead past dizzy heights or cliffs, where one could look sheer down far enough to be dead before he reached the bottom should he fall, and every few feet along the trail of not over a foot in width it would tumble in a foot or so and again take up the original inclination of the mountain, or about that of the leaning tower of Pisa. Here the mule would always be sure to stick one foot over and stumble a little bit, but regain its equilibrium at the next step, having clearly done it intentionally, and for no other purpose than pure maliciousness. One can imagine the cool Alpine zephyr that is wafted up the vertebræ with sufficient force to blow the hair straight up on end. If you have touched the beast within the last three or four days with the whip, or dug into its sides with the spurs when it was absorbed in melancholy reflections, it'll be sure to remember it when you are climbing over the comb of a cliff from two thousand to three thousand feet high, and at the least movement of your feet or twitching of your fingers it will throw its head high in the air, like a hound on the scent, and go stumbling over every pebble and blade of grass on the dangerous way, evidently trying to make you regret that you had ever tried to punish so delicate a creature. At any other time you can turn double somersaults on its back, or act like a raving maniac, and it will not increase its funereal march a foot a day as the result of your actions. Whenever a trail leads exceptionally near a cliff, before it turns on the reverse grade down or up hill, the Mexican mule never fails to go within an inch of the crest and let his leg over with a slight quiver, as he turns around.

All these mountain trails are full of little round, hard stones about the size of marbles, and even larger ones, hidden underneath a carpeting of pine needles. These are liable to make a mule stumble if two feet are on the stones at once, but this is very seldom, although they always go sliding over them on the steeper trails. It is wonderful how these round rocks, hidden under the pine needles on the trail or off it, will throw a human being prostrate if he dismounts a few minutes to take a walk on a slope and stretch his stiffened limbs. Of course the mule, under headway, is liable to walk over him before it can stop or the person pick himself up.

There is another pastime in which the

Mexican mule delights, and in which you won't. It likes to deviate enough to go under every low-branched tree on the trail, and so universal is this trait of char-acter that the trail seems to lead from one low tree or vine to another, just as the mule has a mind to make it. The dodging of limbs and branches among the pines, cypresses, and oaks in the high lands was not so bad, but down in the *tierra caliente* or hot lands, where brambly mesquite and thorny vines were tearing crescents out of your clothes until you looked like a group of Turkish ensigns, it was much more monotonous.

The beast I was compelled to ride had one ear cut off near the head, and looked top-heavy in the extreme. As a mule's ears make up a goodly portion of it, as seen in elevation from the saddle on its back, I was always frightened when he approached a cliff on the unabridged side, and instinctively leaned in to counterpoise the heavy weight that I thought might drag us over the precipice. He was familiarly known by the party as "Old Steamboat," "Old Lumber Yard," and other names indicating these characteristics; but he was large and so was I, and he fell to my lot. When I first saw his abbreviated auricular appendage, as a member of the "Society for the Prevention of Cruelty to Mules," I felt incensed upon hearing that it had been lost by the cut of a whip in the hands of a previous driver; but before we had been acquainted a week I had transferred all my sympathy from the mule to the man, whoever he may have been. On the level ground this mule was slower than the Mexican cook, who took fifteen minutes to wash a spoon ; but on a perilous path of half a foot in width, on a dizzy precipice, the way he could box the compass with the lone ear, so as to catch some faint sound at which he could get frightened at this inopportune time, made me wish I could cut off the other ear at about the third cervical vertebra.

About half-past one on the first day out from Carichic we stopped for our lunch in a grove of beautiful pines in the valley of the Pasigochic, on the banks of a little stream of the same name. As I have said, we had ridden about fifteen miles from Carichic and were all very much in need of rest. Just before lunching we passed a number of Tarahumari Indians of the civilized class, working in a small field of about three or four acres.

Even in this small space there were a dozen others hard at work. Their dark, swarthy bodies were almost the color of the rich soil in which they toiled, making their white breechclouts and white straw hats, the only things they wore, look

A TARAHUMARI MOUNTAIN HOME.

curious enough when they moved about like so many unpoetical ghosts, as seen at a distance.

We were now well into the Sierra Madre range, and although the scenery

was so far about the equal of the Alle-
ghanies or Catskills, there was not much
level ground for cultivation, and this was
eagerly seized by the working natives,
not only to raise crops for their own use,
but to have some to sell; for from six to
seven days' travel to the southwest was
the richest silver district in the world,
where all kinds of produce brought fabulous prices that would have enriched an
American farmer in one season—flour
forty cents a pound and other things in
proportion. Indeed one of the best dis-
tinctions that could be made between the
wild and civilized Tarahumaris is the fact
that the former knows nothing of money
nor makes any attempt to secure it, barter-
ing directly by exchange with the civilized
native for those things he wants and does
not make ; while the latter makes money

his medium of exchange, and seems to thoroughly appreciate its value.

The midday lunch for a party of Mexicans moving through the mountains is quite long by comparison with American parties under like circumstances. It was two hours before we got away again. There are probably two reasons for this, one being that the midday is generally warmer with them than with us, although this did not apply to us in the cool, timbered regions of the high sierras; while the second reason is clearly found in the fact that they seldom feed their mules on these mountain trips, and must give them time to graze a fair-sized meal at noon. The Mexican packs and unpacks the mules twice a day, the American but once; for by feeding grain he can keep going until they want to camp, making it

much earlier than his Mexican brother,
who, starting at three o'clock, has to go
until six or seven to make a respectable
afternoon's march. By three o'clock the
American is generally in camp, having
made the same distance and having done
half the work. It is doubtful, however,
if American mules would do as well here
under like circumstances.

After leaving the pretty and picturesque Pasigochic, a high hill is ascended,
and late that afternoon we passed the
highest point between the morning and
evening camps, eighteen hundred feet.
On the high hills were seen the beautiful madroña tree, or strawberry tree,
with blood-red bark, and bright green
and yellow leaves, and covered with white
blossoms, so startling a mixture of colors
that it would hardly be believed if painted

and put on exhibition. They were everywhere, from the merest bush in size to
trees twenty and thirty feet in height.
In form they are not unlike a spreading
apple tree, with strongly contorted and
twisted branches. Then there were many
oaks of different kinds, the *encino robles*
or everlasting oak, the white oak, and the
little black variety. There were a dozen
kinds I knew nothing of in my limited
vocabulary of forest trees. The pines
were beautiful, and in many places forty
to fifty merchantable trees to the acre,
straight as an arrow, and without a limb
for sixty or seventy feet from the
ground. In one or two clusters I noticed
groups of pines like those an old lumber-
man once pointed out to me in the forests of Oregon as good mast timber. I
have seen the same repeated dozens of

times on the slopes of the Sierra Madre range. This dense mass of spar and mast timber, as I shall call it, is nearly always found on the richest soil of the mountain, generally in the narrow little valleys where the silt from the sides is swept down by the rains until the soil is many feet deep.

The great coniferous forest of the northern part of the Sierra Madre range of Mexico is probably one of the largest in the world (it is undoubtedly the largest virgin forest on either continent), and when its resources are opened by well-constructed wagon roads, or, better still, by a railway system, it will undoubtedly prove an enormous source of revenue to the Mexican States of Chihuahua and Sonora, and to no little extent those of Sinaloa and Durango—a source nearly as

profitable as their mineral wealth, and
this is saying a great deal, for these
States comprise the richest silver district
in the world.

That evening we camped in the valley
of the Guigochic, on another beautiful
mountain stream, where a little park of
an acre or two gave our mules some
sweet alpine grasses, which warranted us
in believing that half the morning would
not be passed in chasing over the hills to
find stray mules, as is so often the case in
Mexico when these beasts are turned loose
to search for their food.    We were all
thoroughly tired with our first day's ride
on mule-back, but nevertheless turned in
to help the cook, as we realized that we
wanted something to eat that night.    The
tent was pitched between two magnificent
pines of enormous size, and I slept to the

music of the wind in their branches. We
left our camp by the light of the camp
fire next morning and started over the
crest of one of the steepest mountains
overlooking our camp. Halfway up the
steep trail we passed two graves of stone
heaps surmounted by rough wooden
crosses. At this spot a man and his wife
had been killed by the Apaches a few
years ago. These same Apaches had
penetrated too far into Tarahumari land,
and after a disastrous encounter with the
latter were fleeing themselves, when they
met the defenseless Mexican and his wife
and killed them. This was the farthest
point west where a white person had been
killed by Apache Indians in this part of
Chihuahua. After climbing this hill of
1500 or 1600 feet our trail still led up-
ward, the mountains growing steeper and

steeper.    When we reached the top of
one peak we would immediately begin
the zigzag descent, then climb up another
and down again.    Sometimes the trail
wound over a bald, rocky peak, where
steps by long years of use had been worn
deep in the soft rock ; and into these little
places the mules would carefully place
their feet, there really being no other foothold for them.    Again there would be a
chain of gigantic stairs leading down
some steep mountain side, where one
could look hundreds of feet, and see tall
trees that from such an elevation re-
sembled small shrubs.    The nimble and
sure-footed animals would place all four
feet together and jump down from one
step to another, oftentimes more than
their own height, so that one felt sure of
being sent flying over the cliff.    Again,

the trail would be over the loose, rolling stones, and the little animals would fairly slide down these dangerous places. By noon we reached the quaint little civilized pueblo of Tarahumari Indians named Naqueachic, they living in rude log houses instead of caves or cliff dwellings.

At the pueblo of Naqueachic of civilized Tarahumaris I found a curious method of cooking. Over the fire the food was boiling in two different dishes. One contained a substance that looked like a compound of mucilage and brick dust. The mademoiselle in charge would take up a calabash gourd full, holding a pint or two, and, although the gourd was held mouth up all the time, before it was three feet above the pot it was completely emptied, so tenacious and stringy was the substance, like the white of a soft boiled egg. This was repeated every five or ten seconds, evidently to keep it from burning. It is made from the soft, pulpy leaves or stalks of the nopal cactus; and is about as palatable to a white man as gruel and sawdust would be. The other pot contained some mixture of corn, beans, and probably one or two other more savage ingredients, a sort of Sierra Madre succotash.

In one corner of the room—I might say the house, for there was only one room in the house—was a rude loom for weaving blankets, which they make from the wool of their mountain sheep, and which under all the circumstances are quite creditable. The ornamentation is not very great, and yet none of them lack this seemingly necessary part of

a blanket.   These blankets are usually of
a dark brown color, with one or two dark
yellow stripes across them at the ends.
Being " all wool and a yard wide " they
are quite warm, much warmer than some
Mexican woolen blankets that I bought
at Chihuahua, which seemed better calcu-
lated to keep the heat out on the cold
nights in the mountains than to keep it in.

The civilized Tarahumaris are quite
cleanly for savages, noticeably more so
than the lower order of Mexicans, and
yet there is plenty of room, great, un-
swept back counties of it, for improvement in this respect.

After leaving the interesting little village of Naqueachic we at once started
over a high range or crest some twenty-
nine hundred feet above our level, and
from the top could look down in a beauti-

ful valley on one of the most important Tarahumari villages in the Sierra Madres, the town of Sisoguichic. I would have

OLD TARAHUMARI INDIAN.

liked to camp here for the night, but as there was no corn for the mules or grass for them to graze on we were compelled to proceed.

# CHAPTER VII.

SOUTHWESTERN CHIHUAHUA—AMONG THE
CAVE AND CLIFF DWELLERS IN THE
HEART OF THE SIERRA MADRE RANGE.

THAT night our camp was in an
immense pine forest on the crest of
one of the high peaks, and here we
parted with our Mexican friend Don
Augustin Becerra, to whom we had
already become deeply indebted, and who
found it necessary to hasten on to his
father's mines at Urique, which we were
to make more leisurely.

There is a widely dispersed variety of
pitch pine in these mountains, which may
be said to be the candles or the lanterns

of the natives of the country. The night scenes in the pitch-pine States of the South have long formed themes in prose and poetry, but those States are in the flat-land coasts of our country, with no scenery to give any of the strange, weird effects of a broken land. At one camp I made upon a high *potrero*, I saw such a scene. It was in a little flat place in the mountain, where the grass was good for the mules, but where the water was far down the precipitous ravine or box cañon that opened out by a gorge to a great barranca as deep and wide as the Grand Cañon of the Colorado. A half-dozen men at a time, all with pitch-pine torches, descended after water, or to drive the mules to and from water. As they cut long slivers of pine, eight to ten feet in length, that blaze for two-thirds to three-

fourths their length, the strange effect on
the wild scenery, stretching for miles, can
be more easily conceived than described.
To have put it faithfully on canvas would
have made the reputation of any artist,
and the equal of which I have never seen.
Vereschagin's "My. Camp in the Himalayas" seemed almost tame by comparison.
The great wide sombreros, glittering
with silver—for even the common peons
of Mexico have more costly hats than the
"Four Hundred" of New York—the
bright red foliage of the manzanillas and
the madroño trees, rendered doubly lurid
by the reflection of the torches, the sharp
rocks of the cañon in battlemented and
castellated confusion, stretching off to the
mighty barranca five thousand to six
thousand feet deep, really made up a
picture that not one painter in a thousand

could have done justice to, and not one could imitate.

On our third day out we crossed a most picturesque stream called the Panascos River. Near the crossing were a number of huge irregular bowlders lying at the foot of a sculptured cliff. Under those that formed cave-like recesses were a number of Tarahumari cave dwellers, looking absolutely comical in their wide-brim straw hats of coarse grass and their primitive breechclouts. Their skins were so dark-colored that had it not been for this white clothing at the two termini it would have been hard to make them out in the dark, deep caverns into which most of them fled upon our approach.

A recently occupied cave of these strange earth-burrowing savages could nearly always be told by the stains of

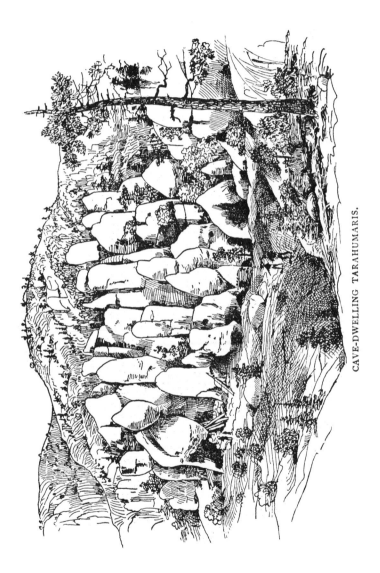

CAVE-DWELLING TARAHUMARIS.

ascending smoke from the highest point
of entrance to the cave.   If the cave has
been abandoned for any length of time
the rain soon wipes out this sure sign of

HOME OF CAVE DWELLERS.

habitation.   We passed a large number
of caves with funnel-shaped smoke stains.
leading up from the outside, but the
silence of death surrounded them, as if
human life had never been within a mile
of the place ; but I have not the remotest

doubt that there were a dozen people inside of each, peeping at us from around the dark corners, having heard our approach and fled in time to keep well out of our sight. Nothing is noisier than a Mexican mule packer, and the mountains are always resounding with his pious shouting to his lazy, plodding animals as he urges them on ; so I considered it very lucky indeed that we saw as many of the living cave and cliff dwellers as we actually did, so excessively shy are these poor, timid creatures.

One of our Mexican packers tried to buy a sheep of one of the civilized Tarahumaris a little farther on, but he would not part with one for any money, although apparently having plenty to spare. Many of the pueblos of the civilized Tarahumaris are really isolated communities, raising all they need for food from the soil, or wool for clothing, or both from animals of the chase, and consequently seldom buying or selling.

That same day we passed La Sierra de los Ojitos. It is a high, shaggy mountain, covered to the very top with a dense forest of pine, and indicates where the waters divide to the east and west. On its slope that we faced, its rivulets poured their contents into the Gulf of Mexico, while from the opposite slope they go into the Pacific Ocean, or rather its great Mexican arm, the Gulf of California. It is the highest point of the Sierra Madres that we encountered on the trail, and I found it to be 12,500 feet above the level of the sea, with La Sierra de los Ojitos towering some 2000 to 3000 feet higher on our left. I camped that night in a picturesque box cañon, which I named Carillo Cajon after the Governor of the State of Chihuahua, who had done a great deal to help the expedition with all the local authorities in the different parts of the State that I might visit. We camped at the first available point we could find, and even here slept at an inclination of some thirty degrees to the level, the mules grazing nearly overhead above us and occasionally rolling a stone down on us during the night.

This part of the Sierra Madres has a great deal of game in it, but the most essential things to hunt it with would be a good pair of wings, things that unfortunately travelers never have. There are many white-tailed deer in the well-wooded valleys. but a brass band would

find them before a Mexican pack train, as
it makes much less noise. In fact this is
true of nearly all kinds of game that can
be frightened off by the lung power of
man. There are also many bears here,
but we saw none, nor any fresh signs of
them. It is said by those who ought to
know that there are two kinds of bears in
the Sierra Madre range, lying between
Chihuahua and Sonora—the common
black species, and a huge brown kind that
must be, I think, the cinnamon or the
grizzly bear, so common farther north.
The Tarahumari natives hunt the deer in
a very singular manner, but they leave
the bears alone, as their weapons, the
bows of mora wood, are not strong
enough for such an uncertain encounter.
The jaguar, or Mexican spotted panther,
is known as far north as this, but

seems to keep to the warm lands, or *tierra caliente*, which restricts it to the low plains of Sonora and Sinaloa, just west of here.

The endurance of these savage sons of the sierras in chasing deer is wonderful. They take a small native dog and starve it for three or four days till it has a most ravenous appetite; then they go deer hunting, and put this keen-nosed, hungry animal on the freshest deer trail they can find. It is perfectly needless to add that he follows it with a vim and energy unknown to full stomachs. Fast as a hungry, starved dog is on a trail that promises a good breakfast, he does not keep far ahead of the swift-footed cliff dweller, who is always close enough behind to render any assistance that may be required if the deer is overtaken or a

fresher trail is run across. I should
say the dog is always liberally rewarded
if the hunt is a success.

If night overtakes the pursuers they
sleep on the trail, and resume the chase
as early next morning as the light will
allow. Once on the trail, however, the
deer is a doomed animal, although the
pursuers have been known to sleep for
two or three nights on its course before
it was overtaken, especially if the fleeing
animal knew in some way that it was pursued long before it was overtaken. Once
overhauled, a series of tactics is begun so
as to divide the labor of the pursuit between the dog and the man, but to give
no corresponding advantage to the deer.
Wide detours are forced upon the deer
by the swift dog, each recurring one being easier to make, and the pursued ani-

mal is brought near the man, who, with loud shouts and demonstrations, heads off the exhausted animal every little while and turns it back on the pursuing dog, until finally in one of the retreats it falls a temporary prey to its canine foe, when the man rushes in and with a knife soon dispatches the game.

Early one morning we could hear wild turkeys calling from one cliff to the other, but as these were over a thousand feet higher and steeper than the leaning tower of Pisa, I suddenly lost all the wild turkey zeal I had brought along with me for the trip. Then, again, if a commander leaves his pack train just as they are getting away, he will surely find a delay of an hour or two on his hands, for which it would take a dozen turkeys to make amends. There is a plentiful sup-

AN OCCUPIED CAVE DWELLING

ply of game in the Mexican sierras, however, for any sportsman who wishes to
devote his attention directly to that
pastime, as shown by the big scores the
natives make when they go on a hunting
trip.

Early next morning we made a start
from our camp on the cañon's side, by
the light of the pitch-pine torches, and
climbed over and out of the deep gorge
into a more open country, where the sun-
light could penetrate. Here the trail
was of velvety softness, and we surprised
a number of cave-dwelling Indians sitting
and standing about their homes among
the big bowlders. The only garments
they had on were ragged breechcloths of
cotton, but some had the extra adorn-
ment of a strip of red cloth about their
shocky black hair. The air was intensely

cold, so much so that we were wrapped in our heaviest coats, but these savages apparently did not feel the cold, and if they shivered at all it was probably at the sight of us—for their fear was quite evident—and it was plain they longed to beat a retreat to their huge rocky homes; but they stood it out till we passed, and then in an instant they vanished.

Before this day's march was ended we passed through a little Tarahumari mountain town called Churo. It was in a small circular valley, and on all sides were the steep, high peaks of the mountains. Here the Indians had tried to raise a few apples, but the trees were gnarled and twisted, and the apples not much larger than those of wild crab trees, although much sweeter to the taste. Of course there was no store of any kind in the lit-

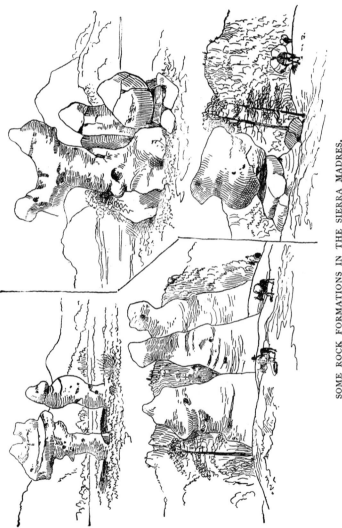

SOME ROCK FORMATIONS IN THE SIERRA MADRES.

tle settlement, and if Mexicans, passing
through the place, wished to obtain anything from the Indians, their method was
to take it, placing whatever they considered its equivalent in silver before the
Indian, and leaving it for the latter to
accept. If asked to sell any of their
produce or set a price on it, the Indians
stolidly refuse, even though the price may
be two or three times greater than they
could possibly obtain at the nearest Mexican mining town. They know nothing
of the value of gold, and paper money
they utterly refuse; silver is the only
money they will take even in this reluctant
fashion.

Upon reaching Cusihuiriachic I found
that my Winchester rifle had been
left in the stage office in Chihuahua.
I sent back word to forward it by next

stage to Carichic, but as the next stage did not arrive at that place for four or five days we would have just that much start of it in the mountains, and we therefore at that place engaged a Tarahumari Indian boy to bring it whenever it did arrive. The gun reached Carichic at noon of one day, and early the next forenoon the young Indian appeared on our trail with it, having made the distance in one night and a little over half a day. Of course he must have used many short cuts across the country of which we were ignorant; nevertheless it was quite a feat, for the distance traveled by us was about 110 miles.

From Carillo Cajon, where our last camp had been, to the westward and southwestward the scenery steadily becomes grander and more mountainous;

TARAHUMARI TOWN OF CHURO.

until the Grand Barranca of the Urique
is reached it fully equals the Grand Cañon
of the Colorado at any point on its course.
Long before, indeed, on our southward
march beautiful vistas break to the right
and the left, and especially to the east.
About five o'clock one afternoon, just as
we were emerging from a dense forest of
high pines, and little thinking of seeing
stupendous scenery, we suddenly came
to the very edge of a cliff fully 1000
feet high, and from which we could look
down 4000 to 5000 feet on as grand a
scene of massive crags, sculptured rock,
and broken barrancas as the eye ever
rested on. It was already late in the
afternoon, so I determined to remain
over a day at this point and devote it
to camera and cañon. This camp on the
picturesque brink of the Grand Bar-

ranca I called Camp Diaz, after Mexico's president.

The Grand Barranca of the Urique is one of the most massive pieces of nature's architecture that the world affords. It is quite similar in some respects to the Grand Cañon of the Colorado, and this is the nearest to which I can compare it in the United States. The latter, grand as the scenery undoubtedly is, soon tires by its monotonous aspect of perpendicular walls in traveling any distance, while the Grand Barranca could be followed as far as it deserves the name of "grand" and every view and every vista would have some startling and attractive change to please the eye. It is a "cross" between the Grand Cañon of the Colorado and the Yosemite Valley—if we can imagine such scenery after seeing both. Were

A VIEW THROUGH ROCK OPENING ACROSS THE GRAND BARRANCA OF THE URIQUE.

the Urique River navigable, fortunes
could easily be made by transportation
lines carrying tourists to and fro, pro-
vided even only one terminus connected
with some well-established line of travel.
But unfortunately it is not navigable, no
amount of money could make it so, and
all tourists or travelers who are afraid of
a little work or roughing it will miss one
of the most magnificent paroramas. It is
simply impossible to crowd into a pen-
and-ink sketch or a photograph any ade-
quate views of this stupendous mountain
scenery. It is rather a field for an artist,
who will put the product of his palette
and brush on heroic-sized canvas, and
make one of the masterpieces of the
world. The heart of the Andes or the
crests of the Himalayas contain no more
sublime scenery than the wild, almost

unknown fastnesses of the Sierra Madres
of Mexico.

From the cliffs we were on, among the
pines and cedars, we could look far down
into the valley of the Urique with our
field glasses and see the great pitahaya
cactus, a product of the tropical climes.
In between were the oaks and other products of temperate climates, showing us
in a huge panorama nearly all the plant
life from the equator to the poles. We
sat on the bold, beetling cliffs, and could
drink ice water from the clear mountain
springs that threw themselves in silvery
cascades below, and view the river far
down in the valley, a perpendicular mile
below us, the waters of which were so
warm that we knew we could bathe in
them with comfort. Away off across the
great cañon were lights, as evening fell,

beaming from the caves of the cliff dwellers on the perpendicular side of the
mountain. Truly it was a strange, wild
sight.

One of the lights that was "raised," as
the sailors would say, in the evening, was
in what seemed to be a perpendicular
cliff on the opposite side of the mighty
barranca, as near as we could make out
in the gloom of the falling night. Its
position was located, and, surely enough,
on the next day our conjectures were
verified, for we could see a few dim
dottings showing caves, while to the
main one led up a steep talus of *débris*
that tapered to a point just in front of
the entrance. Strangest of all, but a
little way down the side of this very
steep talus, so very steep that one would
have had much difficulty in ascending

unless there were brush to assist in climbing, we could easily make out, with the
help of our glasses, that corn had been
planted by these strange people. It
seemed as if the tops of the dwarf plants
were just up to the roots of the next row
of corn above them, if they can really be
said to have been planted in rows at all.

Much as I would have liked to visit the
place, the condition of my mules and the
state of my provisions made it clearly out
of the question; moreover, I was informed that better chances to see cliff
dwellers would present themselves before
long, which statement, fortunately, was
soon verified. Not far from Camp Diaz
was a place where we could have tied our
braided horsehair lariats together and
let a person down one hundred to two
hundred feet into the tops of some tall

pine trees, and from there gain the first
incline, which, though dizzily steep, I
think would have led, by a little Alpine

INTERIOR OF A CLIFF DWELLER'S HOME, SEVENTY-FIVE
FEET ABOVE THE WATER.

engineering, into the bottom of the big
barranca four or five thousand feet below,
and thence an ascent could be made to
the caves of the cliff dwellers. But there

were other and more potent considera-
tions, which I have given, that prevented
our attempting this acrobatic performance
with the cliffs and crags as spectators.
We might say that we were now out of
the land of the living cave dwellers and
in the land of the living cliff dwellers,
although the latter live in caves in the
cliffs.  But I make the distinction between the two, of caves on the level of the
ground in the valleys or the sides of
mountains, and the caves in cliffs or walls.
The latter are reached by notched sticks
used as ladders, or, as I saw in a few
cases, by natural steps in the strata of
alternate hard and soft rock, and up
which nothing but a monkey or a Sierra
Madre cliff dweller could ascend.  Many
of these cliff houses in the caves and
great indentations are one hundred to

FALLS OF THE BECORACHIC, SIERRA MADRE MOUNTAINS,
1239 FEET HIGH.

two hundred feet above the water of some mountain stream, over which they hang like swallows' nests. Truly they are a most wonderful and interesting people, well worth a large volume or two to describe all that is singular and different in them from other people, savage or civilized.

One of the most distinguishing characteristics of the Sierra Madre range, and one that will attract widespread admiration in the near future when this country is better known, is its wonderful rock sculpture. I do not think I exaggerate in saying that I passed hundreds of isolated sculptured rocks in one day. All sketches fail to give an idea of these beautiful formations. They must be seen to afford a conception of their beauty and grotesqueness. Undoubtedly they outrank all other ranges of North

America and, as far as I can learn, of the whole world. Even the Garden of the Gods in Colorado is flat in comparison with some of the many miles of glorious rock formations in these grand old mountains. The trail from Camp Diaz to our fifth camp in the Arroyo de los Angelitos along the western side of the Grand Barranca of the Urique, was as picturesque as the most poetical imagination could conceive. The trail wound up and down the steep arroyos and along the edge of the high cliffs, giving views of unsurpassed beauty and grandeur. That night we slept for the last time under the somber pines and listened to the whip-poor-wills, for the next night we had descended seven thousand feet, and were among the oranges and palms, the paroquets and humming birds.

# CHAPTER VIII.

IN SOUTHWESTERN CHIHUAHUA — DOWN
THE URIQUE BARRANCA—FROM PINE TO
PALM—URIQUE AND ITS MINES.

AS this was to be a most important day
our small party on the crest of one of
the high sierras was astir earlier than usual.
Our camp had been made in a little glen
between two peaks, alongside one of the
numerous clear, cold streams that wind in
and about through all these mountains,
and furnish the loveliest and most
picturesque spots imaginable for camping.
Francisco, my chief packer, a bright,
good-natured Mexican, was off long before sunrise, scouring the ridges and the

gulches for the mules, as these animals
often wander miles away at night, and in
the morning all the available people in
camp are turned out to look for them.
This search sometimes wears well into
the day before these frisky beasts are
brought in ; then some stray human
member of the party has to be found, and
when all this is accomplished it is nearly
time to turn out the mules for another
feed.   On this particular morning fortune
favored us, however, and soon our
dejected-looking beasts were tied in line
with the lariats, while we sat on the
ground a short distance from them, each
with a tin plate in our laps and a tin cup-
ful of coffee in our hands.   The night
before an Indian had arrived at our
camp, sent out from Urique by our
Mexican friend, with roasted chickens and

fresh eggs. The chickens had vanished
on the evening of their arrival, but the
eggs furnished us a royal breakfast with
the usual bill of fare, bacon and coffee.
An early morning in the Sierra Madres,
even in midsummer, will make the teeth
chatter. The only comfort one can get,
after piling on heavy coats, is to pass the
time in revolving about the camp fire just
out of reach of the smoke till breakfast is
ready. Any attempt at washing is sure
to be a failure, for the water is as cold as
ice and the fingers refuse to work in the
frosty air; so it is generally about midday before dirt and the traveler cease to
be companions. After we had thawed
out with the hot coffee, and all the packs
had been strapped on the mules, the
animals were started ahead, with Francisco's assistant, a muscular Indian, run-

ning after them; then the saddles were placed on our worn-out beasts, and off we went with light hearts, for this day's ride was to take us to the large mining village of Urique, buried away in the depths of the Urique Barranca. We had been on the road about an hour, up hill and down dale, crossing innumerable mountain streams, and skirting the edges of precipices from which we caught glimpses of the beautiful valleys thousands of feet below, when we rounded the corner of an immense spur, climbed a high bald point of the mountain, and came suddenly to what appeared to be the end of land. We could now look out for miles into the great mining barranca, broken into innumerable crags and turrets, with ridges and banks of mountains piled high on every side, mountains of purple, red, yellow, and green, magnificent and fantastic, fading away into other barrancas to the right and left. Here we paused, seven thousand feet above the valley, and looked at the wonderful panorama spread before us, celebrated even among these grand old mountains—by the few who have penetrated their fastnesses—as one of the most famous views and formidable descents in the whole range. The guides carefully examined all the packs and saddles, and every strap and rope was tightened and made secure. All were directed to remain in their saddles, as the descent was too steep and the way too dangerous for walking, the path or trail being covered with loose rolling stones. We had been told to give the mules their heads, and trust to their being perfectly sure-footed, for in that respect a Mexican mule is about as certain as a mountain goat.

From " La Cumbra," or the crest of the Sierra Madres, we could look down in the valley of the Urique River, as I have said, something over a vertical mile. As we stood among the pines we could see the plantations of oranges far below, one of which, called " La Naranja "—the Spanish for orange—seemed almost under our feet ; in fact it was not farther away in horizontal measure than it was vertical, or about a mile in both. The Barranca of the Urique was much more open at this point than where we had first struck it at Camp Diaz, but it was, nevertheless, fully as grand and sublime in its mighty scenery, although of quite another kind. The enormous buttresses, almost spurs of mountains, that stood out along the cañon-like sides of the former, with their bristling, perpendicular fronts of thousands of feet in height, were now rounded off along the ridges with their vertical descents, and only their sides were straight up and down. In fact it was down these steep ridges that we must make our descent by zigzag trails that gave us a grade on which a mule could stand. Every time we came to the side of a ridge the trail hung over a precipice with a sickening dizziness to the rider until the mule could make the turn and get back on the descending trail. Occasionally it was necessary to leave one ridge for another far away that gave a better grade, and then we might have to skirt some cumbra, or crest, with walls practically vertical on either side, where, if we ever started to fall, we could guarantee ourselves one thousand five hundred to two thousand feet of plain sailing.

On the trail from Batopilas to Parral is the "La Infinitad" of the Mexican miners (the Infinity), where the trail, not over half a foot wide, looks down a sheer vertical twenty-six hundred feet.

Presently the pines begin to grow less numerous and to be interspersed with the many varieties of oak for which the Sierra Madres will one day be noted, the most conspicuous of which is the *encino robles*, or everlasting oak, a beautiful tree with enormous leaves of a bright green color. The oaks increase in numbers as we descend, and the pines soon disappear; for we are getting out of the country of cold nights, which the conifers love so much. Presently a thorny mesquite is seen, and in half an hour we have traveled

from Montana to Texas, in a climatic
way. On the cumbra we jumped off
from our mules and ran along by the half
hour in the cool, fresh mountain air.
Now five minutes brings out our hand-
kerchiefs to wipe our perspiring brows.
The northern cactus will soon mingle
with the mesquite, and then the great
pitahaya tells us we are on the verge of
the tropics, while each tree in the orange
orchard just below us can be made out,
and after a few more turns on the twist-
ing trails, even the yellow oranges on the
bright green trees become distinct.
Another half hour and we are on the
level, while not that length of time has
been added before palms are over our
head, and the heat is almost unbearable
to those who have been for weeks on the
high mountain tops of the cool sierras.

In a little over four hours we dropped
from the land of the pine to the land of
the palm, and this too on mule-back, a
feat that could be performed in few countries outside of Mexico. We were now
out of the land of wild forests and wild
men, back again among Mexican civilization, but of a kind almost unknown to
the outside world, although one of the
richest mining districts and one of the
oldest points of colonization on the North
American continent.

Our path was now lined with lovely,
flowering, thorny shrubs, that stretched
out and tried to scratch us, and often
succeeded as we passed by. When we
reached the little plateau of the first
orange grove we rested awhile, and from
here could look back to the cool place we
had left but four short hours before.

FROM ORANGE PLANTATION TO CUMBRA, OR CREST OF MOUN-
TAIN, SIX THOUSAND FEET. LOOKING BACKWARD.

The way down from this resting place
seemed steeper and longer than the first
half of the journey ; the heat became intense, the air throbbing and shimmering
in the brilliant sunshine. Gayly colored
paroquets and strange tropical birds went
flitting past us and filled the air with
their noisy calls and cries. The trail,
however, had a persistent, unaccountable
Indian method of keeping away from all
shade, and wound among the thickest
masses of thorny shrubs, which compelled us constantly to keep an eye on
them, or be reminded in a manner more
painful than pleasant. These, and the
intense heat, made me long for the
mountain life again. Although we had
dropped from the crest of the range and
land of pines to the land of palms, seven
thousand feet, still we had many miles to

wind up the great tropical barranca before we would reach the village.

One of the most dangerous places on
the entire trail, about six hundred feet
above the river, was where the mountain
had apparently caved in on a sharp curve.
This cave-in was directly under the trail,
and here it crossed it with an abrupt turn
around the point of the mountain. A
small torrent had cut its way down at
this point, and goats and other animals,
when grazing on the steep slope above,
had loosened quantities of stones and
earth, which had fallen and built out a sort
of ledge or shelf at the same point. This
shelf projected over the great curve in
the hill, and on approaching this place it
looked as if a mule must either walk off
with his fore feet or let his hind ones
drop over the cliff in making the turn.

Of course the trail was as narrow as possible for a trail to be and allow an animal to cling to it.

Through the kindness of Don Augustin Becerra there was sent out from Urique to the orange plantation a very large mule for my personal comfort. This animal was of the pinto variety and a fine traveler. After my desperate encounters with "Old Steamboat" it was positive luxury to ride him. He had some faults, however; he was fresh and fast, so kept well in advance of the rest of the train. When we neared this particularly dangerous place my mule took up a gentle trot and went pounding around the curve in a way that almost turned my hair gray, and I know we all breathed more freely after getting away from the perilous spot.

The Mexican town of Urique, numbering some three thousand people, was first
established in 1612, years before the first
pilgrim landed on Plymouth Rock, and
yet it is as unknown as though in the
interior of Africa. That living cave and
cliff dwellers should be found but a little
way off from the rough and even dangerous trail that leads to the secluded
town which no one troubled himself to
report to the world outside, shows what a
wonderful isolation can exist and still be
called civilization. The only way out of
and into the town was on the back of the
melancholy mule, and an old resident told
me he believed that three-fourths of the
people had never seen a wagon, not even
the wooden carts of the Mexicans that so
remind one of scriptural times ; certainly
no wagon or cart was ever hauled through

URIQUE FROM THE RIVER.

the streets of Urique. In this deep barranca there is just room enough for the
Urique River (a beautiful stream), and
alongside of it, straggling out for a couple
of miles or more, a row of houses hugging the banks of the stream, then a narrow street and a similar row of houses
crowded up on the slope of the mountain. Back of this rise abruptly the steep,
broken crests of the Sierra Madres. On
the opposite side of the river there is
only room now and then for a chance
house that clings to the steep sides of
the hills or burrows into them.

We rode with a great clatter up the
single street lying white and still in the
noonday sun, and had we not known that
preparations had been made for us—as
our arrival was anticipated by Don
Augustin Becerra—we might have mis-

taken the place for a deserted village. After riding a mile through the street we reached a little plaza about twenty-five feet square, where the mountains receded and made room for this level little patch of ground. Here one of the great wooden doors of the apparently deserted houses opened and our host came forth, followed by a number of others. By the time the whole party reached the plaza there were one or two hundred Mexicans congregated to welcome us and see us alight. As there were no accommodations of any sort in the town for travelers, Don Augustin Becerra, with the graceful courtesy of a Mexican gentleman, had moved out of his own home and literally placed his whole house and all it contained at our disposal; and this was done as though it were the most com-

THE ONLY STREET OF URIQUE.

monplace thing in the world, and without
the least sign of ostentatious politeness.
I doubt very much whether any American
under the same circumstances would have
done as much. His father, Don Buena-
ventura Becerra, lived here also, and both
united in showering on us the most ac-
ceptable acts of hospitality during our
whole stay ; and these were doubly welcome, coming as they did in such a spon-
taneous and wholly unexpected manner.

Urique is most interesting in that vast
and substantial mineral wealth of which
the little town is practically the center.
The discovery of the rich district of
Urique is to be attributed, so I am told,
to the "adelantados" or "conquista-
dores," Spanish names equivalent to
"adventurers," and then given to the
commanders of expeditions organized but

a short time after the conquest to explore
the country and extend the domains of the
Spanish crown.   Directly overlooking this
beautiful little mountain town is the Rosario mine, one of the principal mines of the
district.   Its ore runs from two hundred
to two thousand dollars to the ton.   In
fact only the richest ores of any mine can
be worked in the Central Sierra Madres,
where everything is carried for hundreds
of miles on mule-back at rates that would
make a freight agent's mouth water. Salt
for chlorination works, that we get for
five to ten dollars a ton where there are
railways, here costs from one hundred to
one hundred and twenty-five dollars a ton,
and even much more during the rainy
season of about three months, when all
the streams are swollen and the dizzy
mountain trails are dangerous in the ex-

LOOKING DOWN THE URIQUE BARRANCA TOWARD THE RIVER.

treme. This rainy season in Northern Mexico lasts from about the first or middle of June until the middle of September. It is against such enormous odds that man has to battle with Nature in this secluded part of the earth in order to get at her wealth that is otherwise so lavishly strewn around. After one has passed ten or twelve days on the roughest of mountain trails in order to reach this point, and reflects that the discoverers must have been without even this poor aid to progress, one's respect for the old Spanish explorers of the seventeenth century is sure to be heartily accorded. They were undoubtedly a much hardier, more daring, persistent, and intrepid class of people than those who struck the Atlantic shores of our own country. But, great ghost of Cortes, how things have changed!

It seems as if the will and energy of three centuries had been crowded into as many years, and then allowed to stand still, like a watch that loses its balance and spins off the twenty-four hours in nearly as many seconds.

And right here I would refer to the frequent discussion of writers on Mexico as to whether Mexicans are opposed to the introduction of foreign labor and capital to develop their country. All around the town of Urique are to be found mines of gold and silver either operated or about to be operated by Americans, English, Germans, and other foreigners ; while many other enterprises are starting toward this rich country opened by the Spanish before a white man had crossed the Alleghenies. I was therefore in a fair position to hear what their descendants

had to say, and in giving it utterance
let me compare them with our own
countrymen. Individually the Mexican is
never so bitter against foreigners as the
American, although the latter nation is
much more an aggregation of foreigners
than the former, and of much later date
from other countries. I often heard quite
caustic comparisons from sensible Mexicans as to foreign methods of mining,
railroading, etc., which I think were sometimes exaggerative, and they even ex-
pressed opposition to their coming in at
all, but never in a manner so pronounced
as with us.

The whole of the rich Urique district,
formerly an old Spanish grant many
square miles in extent, was granted the
Becerra family of three brothers by the
Mexican Government. Their wealth is

reputed to be many millions, and this we could readily believe while passing through a portion of their vast possessions. There are now in the Urique district a dozen bonanza mines worked by the old Spanish system, which would yield enormous revenues if there were any method by which the ore could be transported at reasonable rates. From almost any point on the one street of the town you could look up the steep mountain sides and see three or four of these old Spanish mines. The method of working them was wholly on the same plan as that adopted a hundred years before, even the machinery being of the most primitive type.

That night I took a swim in the Urique River and found the water as warm as fresh milk, although the water I had used in the morning from some of its small tributaries on the cumbra was as cold as ice.

The post office in the little town was a most curiously primitive affair, being merely an awning of branches held up against a tree by a post in the ground. Under this an old man was seated on a chair ; we saw nothing here to indicate a post office, but were assured this was the spot to deposit our letters. The man regarded me with surprise and distrust, and the sight of the three or four letters I wished to mail drew a large crowd. The old man could not read, and I told him where the letters were to go ; then, after a great deal of jabbering among the crowd regarding the amount of postage, which I fortunately knew and told him, the letters were mailed by being deposited in an empty cigar box at his side, to be handed to the Indian mail carrier on his next trip out of Urique.

Our stay was unexpectedly prolonged by the illness of one of the party. It was the warmest season of the year in the deep tropical barranca, and the change from the cool mountain air of the high sierras was extremely trying to all. We found it was necessary to make an effort to bestir ourselves as far as sightseeing was concerned, but we dared to venture out only after sunset from our comfortable quarters in the thick adobe building. There was no twilight in the great cañon. Almost as soon as the sun disappeared behind the steep mountains darkness came ; but the moonlight nights were simply glorious, transforming the tropical valley into a perfect fairyland ; even the

homely adobe houses were beautiful, and
the most commonplace Mexican, in his
great sombrero with a serape thrown
gracefully over his shoulders, added a
picturesque touch to the scene. Every
available level spot of land in the valley
had been turned by the owners into an
orange grove or a ranch on which to raise
fruits and vegetables for consumption by
their families; and, as all the edible vegetation of nearly every clime grew there,
their tables were always abundantly
supplied.

In wandering along the river bank
I noticed one very effective way the
natives had to protect their gardens from
the intrusions of the small boy or even
smaller animals. On the top of a common adobe fence they planted a row of
the cholla cactus, the most prickly of all

that great family of needles. Even the agile cat could not get over nor around this formidable fence.

We made two ineffectual efforts to get away from Urique before we finally succeeded. In the first instance the packers did not arrive with the mules until noon, thinking by this ruse they would be able to camp in the valley instead of on the mountain, for they much prefer the tropical heat to the chill of the high mountains. The next time they were promptly on hand, but one of the party was too ill to sit up. The third time fortune favored us, and, after bidding adieu to our hospitable friends, we started for the famous Cerro Colorado mine, said to be the richest gold mine in all this part of Mexico. We followed the narrow mule trail that wound along the brawling river, hemmed in on either side by mountains towering three, four, and five thousand feet above us, and were well up the cañon before the first rays of the sun could reach us over the mountain tops. All along the trail the river was lined with beautiful flowering shrubs of every conceivable shade and color. Flitting around among them were brilliantly colored paroquets and many other birds with gay plumage. That morning's ride of ten or twelve miles up the cañon, sheltered as we were from the fierce rays of the sun—which emphasized and reflected the many-colored rocks of the mountains that were carved and sculptured into all beautiful and fantastic shapes—was one of such rare beauty and perfection that even the most graphic pen would despair of doing justice to the subject. About noon we crossed a small branch of the Urique River, for we had turned off from the main cañon into a smaller one, and then started up the steep mountain side. Up the weary mules scrambled and climbed for six long hours, resting now and then while we looked backward and downward at the land of the tropics, all wayside signs of which were fast disappearing. Just before leaving the Urique River we came to a native tannery, which was about as primitive an affair as any we saw in the whole Sierra Madres. For some two hundred yards along the wide river its bottom was white with outstretched hides held there by heavy stones on the upstream corners, and these hides were kept there for weeks to rid them of their hair. Of course we tasted but little of the water below that point. On enormous bent

INDIAN TANNERY ON URIQUE RIVER.

beams at the lower end was found a number of hides stretched, and naked men
scraping them with sharpened stones.
Despite the style of work, the leather
they make is remarkably soft and pliable.
An hour or two before our evening camp
was made we were once more traveling along underneath the shade of the
great somber pines, and the air seemed
cold and unpleasant after our late tropical
experience. As we had no tent with us,
we simply spread our beds upon the soft
pine needles and slept with the stars
shining in our faces. At the first streak
of daylight we were eating our breakfast,
and shortly after were off over the velvety trail that led up the peaks and across
many small barrancas toward the deep
gorge in which was the celebrated Cerro
Colorado mine.

All this portion of the Sierra Madres is unsurpassed for magnificent and thrilling views over dizzy mountain trails. At many places one could look off into infinity from a ledge not over a foot and a half in width on which the mules must walk. Occasionally a steep wall of rock rises many hundreds of feet on one side and along this the mule will carefully scrape. The descent into Cerro Colorado was the most continuous steep I ever saw. Almost before we knew it we were in the tropics again, and that by an incline where, in a dozen places, the uphill rider on one zigzag could, without taking his foot out of the stirrup, kick off the hat of one below him on the other course as he passed.

Cerro Colorado is reputed to be the largest gold mine in the world, and was

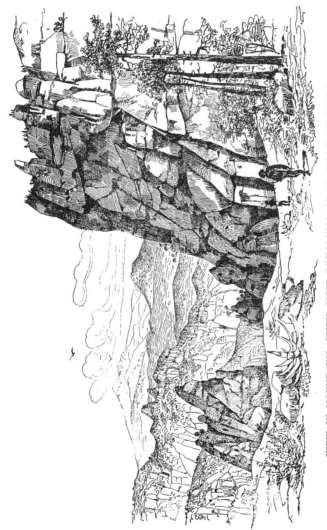

VIEW IN MOUNTAINS, WITH CLIFF DWELLINGS, NEAR CERRO COLORADO.

discovered as recently as 1888. That it
should have remained so long unknown to
any prospector in such a rich silver-min-
ing district is one of the morsels of mining history, even a far greater mystery to
me than that the existence of living cave
and cliff dwellers on the rough mountain trails leading thereto should have
been kept so long quiet. Cliff dwellers
or angels in the air above them, or cave
dwellers or demons in the earth under
them would have attracted but little
attention from a seeker of precious met-
als beyond the momentary astonishment
at their sight.

The Cerro Colorado mine is an immense buttress or spur from the flank of
the Sierra Madres, the whole spur showing signs of gold, not in any distinct
vein, but in great masses distributed here

and there through the mountain, a sort of "pocket" system, as miners would say. This great buttress or spur is 1800 meters (something over a mile) in length, 1200 meters in breadth, and 500 meters in height, and runs from $1 to $3300 a ton, as would be expected in the pocket system of deposits. Small deposits have been found of one hundred weight or so, however, that would run enormously—over $100,000 to the ton. The gold is not wholly in pockets, for it is found distributed in all parts of the great red hill, at least in the minimum of one dollar per ton. It requires eight mines to cover the tract properly. Enormous works were being put in to develop the property, and in a few years it will be known whether this is the largest gold mine in the world or not. It is the property of the Becerra brothers, and when I visited it Don José Maria Becerra was at the mine and spared no pains to make my stay pleasant. He was then engaged in placing the most improved machinery and constructing enormous works for water power, etc. He brought out and laid on a chair four great lumps of gold, of about the value of seventy thousand dollars, that had just been run out by the Mexican *arastra*, for they were still using the ancient method of mining, awaiting the arrival of the new machinery. Our host was preparing to start for London and Paris on business connected with his mine, and when we again heard of him it was the sad news of his death in London. This was not only a severe loss to his family, but a great blow to that portion of the country where his progressive energy had done so much to further its development.

# CHAPTER IX.

SOUTHWESTERN CHIHUAHUA—DESCRIPTION
OF ONE OF THE RICHEST SILVER REGIONS
OF THE WORLD—MINERAL WEALTH OF
THE SIERRA MADRES—THE BATOPILAS
DISTRICT.

AFTER leaving Cerro Colorado, with
its undeveloped possibilities, the
trail leads southwestward through the
broken barrancas toward Batopilas. This
portion of the trail has been so improved
by the energetic mine owners, and was so
broad and smooth, that our mules could
often take up a trot, which seemed doubly
fast after our laborious plodding through
the rough, unbroken portion over which
we had passed. This trail had been built

along some of the steepest cliffs and most
rugged mountain sides, and must have
been a work of great expense, for after
every rainy season, lasting from June till
September, these are badly washed out
and require continuous repairs. The
usual Mexican method is to abandon a
badly washed trail and strike out in a new
direction. Thus one finds all sorts of
paths in the mountains, and it is necessary
to have a good guide who knows the way
thoroughly, or bring up suddenly on the
washed-out ledge of an unused trail and
then retrace your steps to its junction
with another. Long before we reached
Batopilas we came upon some of the
massive work being constructed at that
point, and were in a measure prepared for
the energetic American activity, but not
for the castle-like structure, the hacienda

of San Miguel and San Antonio, as the home of ex-Governor Shepherd, the part owner and superintendent of those famous mines is called. Entering through a massive stone archway, we passed by some of the principal offices within the inclosure, and then on to the residence portion of the great conglomeration of buildings. Here our welcome was of the heartiest description, and everything possible was done for our comfort and pleasure. The great buildings were lighted by electricity and furnished with all modern conveniences, including hot and cold water, steam baths, and, an unusual luxury, an immense swimming pool, formed by a slight deflection of a portion of the Batopilas River. The many comforts of this place made us loath to leave it for the mountain trail.

I shall try and give my readers some slight idea of the wealth of this portion of a country so famous in early Spanish conquest. In those great, broken barrancas, leading out to the westward from the heart of the Central Sierra Madres, I found myself in the richest mineral district of America, and probably the richest in the world. The fact that this is not generally known (and, to tell the truth, bnt very little has ever been published in the English language about so rich a district, and that little is very old) would make it easy to write a book on this region alone, and still leave a great deal unsaid. One of the late cyclopedias says of Mexican mines, " Almost one-half of the total yield [of silver] is derived from the three great mining districts in Guanajuato, Zacatecas, and Catorce."

Like most cyclopedias, this one was a little late in its information when printed, although it had an inkling of the truth in saying: " The State of Sinaloa is said to be literally covered with silver mines. Scientific explorers who visited the Sinaloa mines in 1872 reported that those on the Pacific slope would be the great source of the supply of silver for the next century." The fact is that the center of the greatest source of supply has moved even north of Sinaloa, to about the boundary line between the States of Chihuahua and Sonora, and about one-third of the way from its southern end. Taking either Batopilas or Urique as a base, and with a radius of 180 or 200 miles, that is, a diameter of 400 miles on them as a center, there is no doubt that the resulting circle will include the richest mining district in America, and probably in the world, both in a present and pro-spective sense. From within that circle comes a little over one-fourth the bullion of the whole of Mexico, although this area is insignificant compared with all the territory of that celebrated republic.

In 1864 a report of the mines of Mex-ico was expressly made for Napoleon III. by Dr. Roger Dubois, the French consul. He said as follows of those of Western Chihuahua: "Of all the States of the Mexican Republic, Chihuahua is, without contradiction, the richest in minerals, and we count no less than three thousand dif-ferent leads, the greater part of which are silver." Probably three or four times that number could be added to Dr. Du-bois' estimate of just a quarter of a cen-tury ago to bring it up to the present

date, all of the new mines being in the
Sierra Madres, where not one in a hundred can be worked unless of fabulous
richness. One of the new railways projected into this part of Mexico made
a most thorough examination of this
mining belt to see what could be depended on for freight, and their chief
engineer told me that no less than two
thousand mines of silver that do not pay
now could be made to do so by the cheap
transportation of a railway. If one will
reflect that there are now in the whole
of Mexico but 1247 mines being worked
(gold, silver, copper, lead, tin, and cinna-
bar), it is easy to see that my statement
of this being the richest mining district
of Mexico, and therefore of America,
will admit of no doubt, and especially in
a prospective sense. Already, in antici-

pation of a railway, many large companies are prospecting their concessions, while the individual miner is also to be found with pickax, pan, and shovel on his back, making for this El Dorado, so old in many ways, and yet so very new.

Mr. H. H. Porter, the prospecting engineer of the Batopilas Mining Company, told me, and showed me the various specimens to verify his statement, that in one little area three hundred yards square, there were found twelve veins of silver running from three dollars to seventy-eight dollars to the ton. The reader unacquainted with mining may understand this by my saying that any silver mine of over twenty dollars to the ton is a fortune to its owner if on or near a railway. There are over five hundred veins in the Batopilas concession of sixty-four square miles, and should any new railway running near by justify further research, it could probably be made five thousand without much trouble.

The history of the big Batopilas Mining Company, about the center of the district I have spoken of, and which stands head and shoulders above all the surrounding mining companies, is a fair example of all in this part of the country where my travels were cast.

Batopilas, or Real de San Pedro de Batopilas, as it was originally named, is said to have been discovered in October, 1632. Like Urique, its discovery is to be ascribed to the "adelantados" sent out shortly after the conquest to explore the country and enlarge the possessions of Spain. It is surmised that the rich mineral finds made near the capital, and which subsequently extended far into the interior, led to the progress of the "adelantados" further north, and inspired the expedition into the Sierra Madres which gave rise to the discovery of Batopilas. Tradition has it that upon their descent to the river bottom the "adelantados" were struck by the luminous appearance of the rocks, which were covered in many parts by snowy flakes of native silver. Hence the name "Nevada," signifying "a fall of snow," which was applied to the first mine worked in the district. The news of the discovery spread far and wide, and, as the evidence of its great richness multiplied, it soon became one of the most famous mines of New Spain. The first miners of the new discovery made a magnificent present to the viceroy, composed entirely of large pieces of native silver, the richness of the ore being unprecedented. I have now in my possession ore from Batopilas that runs from six thousand to eight thousand dollars to the ton, and that looks like a mass of solid silver ten-penny nails imperfectly fused together; so I can readily see how the present of solid native silver could have been made.

In 1790 a royal decree ordered the collection of all data for a history of New Spain, and a special commission of scientists was ordered by the viceroy and Royal Tribunal of Mines to report upon the Batopilas district. There is but one copy of the report extant, which I traced to the city of Chihuahua. The commission states that the silver extracted from Batopilas in a few years amounted to fifty million dollars, not including that which was surreptitiously taken out to escape the heavy imposts levied by the crown, and which must have been enormous. The most famous period of "bonanza" for the Batopilas district was during the last fifty years of the eighteenth and the first years of the present century. During this time the famous mines of Pastrana, El Carmen, Arbitrios, and San Antonio were discovered, and yielded the fabulous returns which have been variously estimated at from sixty million to eighty million dollars. From the outset of the Mexican Revolution in 1810 a period of decay set in, which reduced Batopilas greatly and almost caused its ruin. The many revolutions, together with the wonderful discoveries of very rich gold and silver mining districts adjoining this one, depopulated it to such a degree that it counted but ten resident families in 1845. From this time the reaction which has made Batopilas the richest silver district in the world may be said to date. The old mines were again opened and new ones discovered. The measure of success did not compare with that attained in the time of the Spaniards, however, owing to the lesser energy displayed, but proved amply sufficient to repay the timid efforts of the native speculators.

Not until the year 1862 did American enterprise direct its efforts in so promising a direction. A purchase was effected by an American company, composed principally of gentlemen interested in Wells, Fargo & Co., whereby the property embracing the famous veins of San Antonio and El Carmen passed into

their hands.   They operated with great
success in the face of many difficulties
until the year 1879, when the property
again changed hands, and was acquired
by a stock company, which has held
and worked it to the present day.   The
American companies in this, the richest
mining district in the world, are :   The
Batopilas Mining Company, the Todos
Santos Silver Mining Company, and the
Santo Domingo Silver Mining Company.
The Mexican mining companies are quite
numerous, as may be supposed, but I
shall not detail them, as it would require
too much space.   Many of them are very
important, as the Urique and Cerro Colorado companies.   Altogether there are
over a hundred in a greater or less degree of active operation in this rich district, all contained within a radius of four

miles. Of these the Batopilas Mining Company owns and operates over sixty. It is without doubt one of the most important American mining ventures in Mexico. It is also a mining company that has had great difficulties to contend with. Its isolation in the establishment of a business of such magnitude in the heart of the Sierra Madres in so short a number of years is an accomplishment suggestive of great energy. This company owns nearly all the famous old mines in this district which, in the times of the Spaniards, yielded those fabulous bonanzas that caused the astonishment of the world. It has had to repair the follies which, from a scientific standpoint, were committed by several generations of inexpert and short-sighted Mexican mine owners. It has had to clear the old mines of immense masses of rock and dirt which had accumulated during many decades of abandonment, "gutting and scalping," as the miners say. Recently over one hundred miles of openings have been made. The most important is the great Porfirio Diaz tunnel, to be 3½ miles in length when completed—one of the long-est and most important mining tunnels in the world, cutting over sixty well-known veins at the river's level. No one can look at the great mills, the aque-duct of enormous masonry (eight or nine miles long, and that will take up all the water of the Batopi-las river), or the town of Batopilas (a most active place of six thousand people) without respecting the energy that has accomplished all this. The history of

Batopilas is only the history of many other mining districts throughout this country, and the fortunes taken from these mines, and those still behind in them, seem unreal and bordering on romance.

There is one mine near the city of Chihuahua, the Santa Eulalia, which in days gone by built the fine cathedral at that place at a cost of eight hundred thousand dollars. This was done by simply paying a tax of about twenty-five cents on every pound of silver mined, which was ample atonement for any or all sins that the owners could commit.

From Batopilas, north or south, the mighty range of mountains lowers in height, while the big barrancas do not cut so deep into their flanks anywhere else as here, giving the finest Alpine scenery to be found in this part of the continent.

Some of the outside facts regarding the mines are really more interesting than the mines themselves. The miners work in the hot interiors bare to the skin, except their sandals and a breechcloth. Even these have to be examined when they emerge from the mine after the work is over. The sandals are taken off and beaten together, while the breechcloth is treated in the same manner if the examiner demands it. Of course the miners are usually known to the examiner, and his searches vary with the supposed honesty of the different workmen. In a mine where pure silver has been known to be cut out with cold chisels by the mule load, and sent direct to the retorts for smelting, the temptation was very great to purloin a little with each departure from the mine ; and accounts of the sly efforts of some of the thieves appear more like the yarns in detective stories than cold facts. Ventilating tubes, small as gas pipe and covered with wire gauze, have been used to transfer the metal from the interior to the exterior of the mine for quite long distances. Imitation kits of tools have been made of drills, hammers, etc., all of which were hollow and used for stuffing in stray bits of solid silver. Even candles and candle holders were made hollow and thus used for stealing. I could give a dozen other most singular means employed by these miners in their pilferings.

The tunneling of the old Spaniards was very slow compared with that now done by machinery. In some places there were evidences that they had heated the stones by fire and had then thrown water thereon, shivering the front by sudden chilling, a method yet employed in Honduras and Guatemala, according to an engineer at Batopilas who had recently arrived from those countries.

One of the most singular things connected with prospecting in this particular portion of the mountains is the means by which large deposits of silver near a tunnel can be located. If an iridescent, smoke-like appearance spreads over the rocks at any point of a new tunnel or drift at the end of a week or two, the engineers always drift for it and generally strike silver. This stain is called by them " silver smoke," and is

said to be unknown in any other mines.
I was given a half dozen theories in re-
gard to it, mostly of a chemical character,
but the mere fact that such a strange condition exists to help man pry into nature's
secrets is more interesting than any explanation.

From the garden of the hacienda,
surrounded by banana and orange groves
and all kinds of tropical plants and
flowers, one can look up the steep sides
of the mountains, which rise abruptly on
both sides, to the oaks and pines beyond,
and, while sitting on the veranda sipping
ices or drinking cool and refreshing
drinks, and vigorously using the fan,
realize that only a mile above, on the
cumbra or crest of the steep mountain,
the ice water flows freely in the little
mountain streams and the heaviest

flannels only would be comfortable.

My stay at Batopilas was somewhat prolonged in waiting for a party that was soon to descend with bullion to Chihuahua. I had originally intended to continue my course toward the Pacific, but the hot weather, more severe in May and June than during July and August, owing to the rainy season tempering the latter, and the fact that I could find a more interesting trip through the Sierra Madres by another trail than that by which I had entered, determined me to turn my face eastward and keep on the high plateau with its grand equable climate. In leaving Batopilas the large pack train carrying the bullion was given two days' start, and we were to ride and join them after they had made the cumbra or crest of the mountains. This trail took me well to the southward of the one traversed on entering the mountains, and gave me a new and interesting country.

On the high mountain crest between Urique and Batopilas I had gained my furthest point west. The Sierra Madres break more abruptly on their westward slopes, and from the crest we could make out the great plains of Sinaloa and Sonora stretching far away toward the Gulf of California. The country to the west in Sonora and Northern Sinaloa is one of the most fertile in Mexico. The valleys of the Fuerte, the Mayo, and the Yaqui are as rich as any river valleys in North America, and perfectly susceptible of sustaining a dense population, or will be when all the Indian troubles of that region are definitely settled. Most of the crops are of the kind, however, that need cheap transportation to compete with less favored districts in the markets of the world, and are now restricted in amount to what is necessary for a mere local consumption. Here wheat yields enormously to the acre, and the fields are so dense that it is next to impossible to wade through them. Cotton grows more luxuriantly than anywhere on the North American continent. Cotton is planted here oftentimes only once in many years, and large fields are seen four, five, and even seven years old, yielding two and three crops annually. In the same field can be seen plants in blossom, pods, and ripe cotton being picked. It will be one of the leading cotton districts of the world when a railway cuts through it so that the producer can have some show to compete with other districts. Corn is very prolific, coffee produces well, tobacco is of fine flavor, and oranges, guavas, bananas, and

INDIAN WOMAN GRINDING CORN.

plantains are plentiful and of rich flavor ; but transportation on a pack mule for 100 or 200 miles is,too uncertain as to condition of delivery, and too certain as to exorbitant price, to encourage their cultivation beyond local needs of a limited amount. The Fuerte (in Spanish meaning "strong") is a strong-flowing river with enough water—as its name would indicate—to irrigate both sides of its course for nine or ten miles in width. The Mayo is but little inferior, and the Yaqui is even greater.

The Pacific ports of this fertile belt are Mazatlan, Guaymas, and Topolobampo. At the latter point an American colony was founded some years ago, of which the reading public heard considerable, not very favorable to that country as a colonization district, and with a great deal of aspersion thrown at the colonizers. There was so much crimination and re-crimination by the two sides that I do not believe anybody ever obtained a clear idea of how matters stood there. The fact is about this : A colony was put in

a part of an extremely rich country with
the ultimate expectation that a railway
would be completed from that point to
the Rio Grande and to Eastern connec-

A CIVILIZED TARAHUMARI COOKING.

tions. Had the railway been finished,
every colonist with enough gray matter
in his brain to know his way home would
have made a competence at least, and
probably a fortune. This is just as sure
as that fortunes have elsewhere been

made through the development by railways of new, rich countries.  But with its
failure there was no halfway ground to
stand on, so that in this instance there
arose such an amount of misty accusa-
tion and rejoinder that many people in
an indefinite way laid all the blame on
the country; a most erroneous conclusion.
When a railway is completed through
this country there will be the usual
amount of money made that such circumstances justify, but only by those who
have selected the right time for it.

As I have already said, the main portion of the large pack train was started
ahead to give it an opportunity to rest
a little before attempting to climb the
steep mountain trail, and, after reaching
the cumbra, or crest, another breath-
ing spell before starting on their long

journey. It was now nearing the rainy
season, and even if we made haste we
would only just escape this unpleasant
and rather dangerous time in the high
sierras, for there the floods pour down
and often carry out large portions of the
trail on the steep and narrow mountain
passes. Our pack train consisted, all
told, of about seventy or eighty mules,
twenty to thirty of them loaded with
silver bricks for Chihuahua, the rest of
the train being the pack and riding
mules of the various drivers and attendants of the "conductor," as the principal
personage in charge of the bullion is
called.

This person was an immense quadroon,
a person of unusual executive ability in
that position, and thoroughly trusted by
the superintendent, ex-Governor Alex-

ander Shepherd. He had under him a half dozen able assistants, all Mexicans, and was accompanied by three or four "valiantes," as they are called, men of renowned prowess, who have at least "killed their man," and who could be relied on to protect the train in case of attack by robbers. As this large cavalcade moved off up the narrow barranca or cañon it presented a motley and picturesque appearance from its gayly dressed and heavily armed attendants, well mounted on their sturdy mules, to the Indian drivers, with only a blanket apiece for covering and a stout stick to help them over the ground. Even the most civilized of these Indians think nothing of such a walk, two or three hundred miles, resting every night as they do when in attendance on a large

A GOATHERD'S CACHE IN THE MOUNTAINS.

pack train and sharing in the good food supplied them by the owner. Indeed it is really a treat to them. Among the Indian drivers were two or three who had never seen a railway, nor had they ever visited a city as large as Chihuahua, and they were looking forward with feverish anxiety to this great event of their lives. They had heard of the wonderful Mexican Central Railway and the great trains of cars that moved so fast, but their minds seemed filled with unbelief until they could really take it in for themselves. The semi-civilized or civilized Tarahumari Indians are the best natured people imaginable, and there is nothing they are not willing or anxious to do for you if in your employ. They possess the same docile obedience and fondness that a dog exhibits for his

master, and are constantly anticipat-
ing little wants and looking for little
favors they can do you, and this too
without expecting any reward whatever.

# CHAPTER X.

AFTER bidding adieu to our hospitable host and the many friends at the great hacienda, we started quite late in the afternoon to ride about eight or nine miles up the Batopilas River to a station of the Batopilas Mining Company called the Potrero. On either side the Batopilas lifts its banks from four to five and even to six thousand feet above the river bed, making a wonderfully beautiful panorama of rugged mountain scenery as you wind along, sometimes climb-

345

ing up a few hundred feet and then descending to the water's edge to cross at some favorable ford. For the cañon through its entire length is very narrow, and in some places there is only room for the rushing river with the trail hugging the banks or finding a foothold for the mules on the steep, broken mountain side. I hardly know which looks the more impressive, to stand upon the crest of a high cañon or to wind through its depths and look up at its beetling sides, which seem to cleave the clouds. Whatever be the point of view, from top or bottom, with the usual discontent of human beings in all things, the observer will always wish he were at the other place, from which, as he imagines, something better could be seen.

At the Potrero I found a good, sub-

stantial log house, built and maintained
by the Batopilas Company, and used
by them as a shelter for members of
their pack trains, instead of depend-
ing on the sky for a covering. One
end of the house was divided off, where
grain was stored for all the animals.
There was also a storeroom for provisions of various kinds, thus saving
much packing over the rough mountain
trail.

These houses, I learned, had been
built about every thirty-five miles along
the trail, and at each a trusty Indian lived
to care for them. They were a great
comfort, and seemed even luxurious after
a hard all-day ride on the rough trail.
At each was a large corral or pen, into
which the mules were turned for their
feed, and this too was a saving of labor

and time to the packers, and allowed one to make a much earlier start, as well as to omit the long noon camp of the Mexicans. In each of the houses was an immense fireplace, which, on the arrival of the party, was piled with pitch-pine, and a most welcome blaze and warmth soon thawed out the coldest.

At the Potrero a church, built by the first Jesuits in this country, still remains, and is used for devotion by the Indians, although roofless and over two hundred years old. Standing near the ruined door, and looking in, one sees an altar surmounted by a cross and a scaffolding of flowers. Above this is one of the most beautiful pictures ever seen in such a peculiar framing. The roofless old church reveals the most magnificent castellated cliffs to be seen along the

Batopilas River for many miles. Taking
the tops of the battlements, which rise
thousands of feet in sheer altitude in
many places, so that they will fall just
below the top of the church door, thus
leaving a little streak of blue sky between,
and viewing the scene as framed by the
rest of the church, the observer has a
picture before him that would make the
reputation of any artist who could transfer it to canvas with reasonable ability.
Near by was the primitive belfry, two
sticks set in the ground, and the bell, an
old bronze one, hung from a cross-piece
between them. Once each year a priest
visited this place, upon which occasion a
great festival was held. Indian runners
were sent out into the mountains for
many miles around, to induce the timid
Tarahumaris to come in. Here all the

civilized and semi-civilized brought their
children to be christened, and they again
induced many of the wilder Indians of
the cliffs and caves to join them.   In this
way the priests reach the wilder ones, and
sometimes conversions are made among
them.  This is their only method of
approaching   the   uncivilized   natives,
through the medium of those not quite so
wild, who allow them to visit their homes
in the cliffs and crags and hold a limited
intercourse.   From the steep cliffs above
the resort, the wild Tarahumaris can look
down on the strange doings of their more
civilized brothers in the little valley below.   This they told us was often done,
but the instances were quite rare in which
the very wild ones had been coaxed down
from the crags above.

I have been asked what chance a missionary would have among these people and how he could best reach them. Where the patient priest or Jesuit fails to penetrate with all the assistance he can derive from those of his own faith who are kinsmen of the people to be approached, it would seem indeed a difficult task for those of other beliefs.

I was told that these people, the semi-civilized Tarahumaris, are particularly fond of colored prints, and any brightly colored picture is to them an object of veneration. Often old copies of *Puck* or *Judge* drift down here, passing from the hands of miners to Mexicans and thence to the Indians. These they preserve and worship as saints, and to them they offer up their simple prayers.

Early the next morning we were to climb to the top of the steep cliffs behind the old church at the Potrero ; that night we slept for the last time in the land of the tropics.    Late in the evening I walked over by the home of a Tarahumari Indian,   He had a bright fire burning in front of his hut, and on the ground his family were all sleeping peacefully, even down to a very young baby. The house appeared to be deserted, being used probably only during the rainy season.

Next morning by four o'clock we began the ascent of the steep mountain.    It was before daylight when we left the cañon, and by the time we had climbed for three hours I noticed one of the most singular cliff or cave dwellings I had so far seen. There was a distinct trail leading to it. This trail could be perceived from the very bottom of a deep cañon which

CLIFF DWELLING IN A CAÑON LEADING OUT FROM THE BATOPILAS BARRANCA.

branched off from the Batopilas, led along dizzy cliffs, holding to the sides of the steep mountain until it reached a height fully equal to our own, and finally disappeared in an enormous cave. This must have been capable of containing hundreds of people, as it was over a mile distant, and at that distance we could perfectly discern its mouth and even its interior walls. It was the dizziest climb to a home I have ever read of or seen.

That afternoon I came to the farms of some civilized Tarahumaris, built on the very steep mountain side, on which the dirt was held back by terraces or rude retaining walls, so very similar to those seen around the ruins of Northwestern Chihuahua, supposed to be Toltec or Aztec, that I could not help thinking that there was some closer connection between them than that of mere resemblance.

I had heard a dozen theories to account for these terraces in the North, as for collecting water in dry seasons, for conducting water, as places for defense, etc., etc., but, with an actual case directly under observation, this seems to be a better explanation : In decades and centuries of rainy seasons of more or less violence, after the people had abandoned these northern houses, or had been killed by their enemies, all the retained loose earth would have been swept away, leaving only rude and dilapidated walls or terraces sweeping around the mountain sides, from which almost anything could be inferred, whether the most peaceful form or the most warlike fortification.

Although our journey began at four

o'clock in the morning it was two or three
o'clock in the afternoon before we reached
the welcome shelter of the next station,
and it seemed to me from beginning to
end one uninterrupted climb.    This station on the Teboreachic was an exception
to the rest on the trail regarding distance,
for it is only eighteen miles from the Potrero, although eighteen miles of incessant
uphill work.   While the trail is by no
means as steep or dangerous as that leading into the Urique barranca, it is fully as
long a climb to reach the top or cumbra,
and one does not welcome a retreat to
the somber pines with half the enthusi-
asm inspired by a descent into the tropical
foliage of the deep barrancas.   I have
already described so many ascents and
descents, that carried us from one kind of
climate to another, that I hardly think it

necessary to repeat it in this instance. One feature of the ascent, however, exceptionally pleasant, was the ease with which one could get off one's tired mule and not only earn its gratitude, if a mule may be said to possess that virtue, but also stretch one's weary limbs by climbing over a comparatively good trail.

As soon as we were well up in the mountains we found the region extremely well watered, beautiful streams flowing through every little glen or valley, many of them filled with small trout. This Batopilas trail differed from the other in that some attempt at grade had been made. It did not adopt the erratic Indian method of making for the top of every tall peak and then climbing down on the other side, only to repeat the performance until the rider became almost seasick from the

undulations. Since Batopilas came into
the hands of Americans there has been
a constant effort on their part to look
for better grades and secure a simpler
method of ingress and egress from their
mountain mines, and they are continually
broadening and improving the path.
Still, at the best, they can never make
anything but a narrow mountain trail in
that country of crag and cañon. The
day will come when railways are built
through that rich region, but until then
the patient mule will be the only means
of transportation.

The first night on the Teboreachic
was a most delightfully cool one after
the long spell of warm weather we had
experienced on the lower levels. It was
preceded by a slight thunder shower, the
first one of the season, but it warned us in

unmistakable terms that the rainy season
was not far off, and that we had better
get out of the mountains before it was
upon us.  Before making La Laja, the
second night, we passed the homes of
many Indians, both of the semi-civilized
type and the wilder ones of the cliffs and
caves.  At one point I stopped to get a
photograph of the homes of some cliff
dwellers, where, directly below the cliffs,
were a couple of rude stone huts, built on
a steep side of the mountain.  The men
seemed to be absent from this place, but
we could see the forms of some women
moving about and crouching down to
avoid being seen by us.  My Mexican
man, Dionisio, was greatly alarmed at
my action in dropping behind the party
to photograph this group of strange
homes, and loudly declared we would all

HOMES OF SEMI-CIVILIZED TARAHUMARIS.

be shot by the men, should they return and see us at this, to them, strange work. It was almost impossible to induce Dionisio to bring up my camera or hold my mule, so anxious was he to get away. There was really no danger whatever from these people, as they only fight to defend their homes, but the fear of the cowardly Mexican was very amusing.

Before leaving Batopilas we had been told that whatever we had seen of the wonderful or beautiful in nature on our outward journey by other trails, a treat of a most magnificent character was reserved for us on this route, one that was unique and wholly without parallel in those grand old mountains. This was the day's journey through the Arroyo de las Iglesias. So we were in a measure prepared for the many beautiful sights that awaited

us on our third day. Although we had
been passing through picturesque valleys
and were constantly crossing lovely
mountain brooks, one must admit without
hesitation that of the many hundreds of
beautiful streams in the Sierra Madre
Mountains, flanked by cut and carved
stone, there is none that will compare in
extent or beauty with the sculptured rock
of the Arroyo de las Iglesias (the Cañon
of the Churches), so named on account of
the spires of rock that greet one on every
side for the greater part of a day's travel.
For eighteen or twenty miles the Cañon
of the Churches seems more like some
theatrical representation of a fairy scene
than a real one from nature. The limestone has been eroded into a thousand
fantastic forms by the action of the
elements, the predominating one being

some feature of a church or cathedral, either in spires, minarets, or flying buttresses built far out from the main walls of the cañon. The most grotesque forms are those that generally cap the spires; it seems necessary that some hard rock above should protect the softer underneath in order to insure one of these petrified pinnacles of nature.

One of them, two hundred feet in height, as seen from the cañon, was as good a spread eagle as a person would want to see cut out of stone, while on a tower not a hundred yards away was a bust of Hadrian, quite as good as that in the Metropolitan Museum of Art, ten times as large, and a thousandfold more conspicuously placed. A person with a small amount of imagination could easily make a land of enchantment out of this

*arroyo* with its singular columns and pillars, its leaning towers and busts and
statues, that meet him on every side and
are repeated every few hundred yards by
great cañons that break off to the right
and left, and which are perfect duplicates
of the original through which the traveler wends his way.

Strange, singular, and curious as are
these works of nature, they are not so
astonishing to the average civilized person as the works of man. Among these
beetling crags and dizzy cliffs savage
men have found places to erect their
houses and live their lives. Ladders of
notched sticks lead from one crag to the
crest of another, whenever the rude steps
made by nature do not allow these creatures of the cliffs to climb their almost
perpendicular faces; a false step on the

HOMES OF CLIFF DWELLERS IN ARROYO DE LAS IGLESIAS.

slight ladders or a turning of one of
them, which to me seemed so likely,
would send the climber two hundred to
three hundred feet to the bottom of the
cañon, perhaps a mangled corpse.

Had I wanted to visit them directly in
their homes I doubt very much if I could
have reached them, for I am sorry to
say I am not a sailor, a tight-rope per-
former, or an aëronaut. Beyond this
place the people had fled to their houses,
and could, by disarranging a single
notched stick, have made our ascent impossible. This, I think, was one of the
methods of defense adopted by ancient
cliff dwellers of Arizona, as shown at
least by some which I have seen and
which now, with the logs rotted away,
are unapproachable. It is even possible,
as I have more than hinted before, that

there is some closer affinity between the Arizona and Mexican cliff dwellers than this simple but suggestive one I have mentioned. It is certainly a question I would like to see some good archæologist struggle with for a year or two.

So steep are the walls of the Arroyo de las Iglesias in many places where we observed cliff dwellers that, had they thrown an object from the little porthole-like window of their stone pens with ordinary strength, it would certainly have brought up in the cañon bottom probably two hundred or three hundred feet below. How they can rear little children on these cliffs without a loss of one hundred per cent. annually is to me one of the most mysterious things connected with these strange people.

They are worshipers of the sun, so

IN ARROYO DE LAS IGLESIAS, CLIFF DWELLINGS IN ROCKS.

good authorities say, and on the first day
of a child's life they dedicate it to that
great orb by placing it in his direct rays.
In many other ways they show their devotion. to that source which has been
loved by so many primitive people.
Their whole range of worship would
certainly be interesting in the extreme.
They have the greatest dread of the owl,
which, as is known elsewhere as well as
here, has some association or other of
evil connected with it, from the slightest
disaster to death. How many other
things they fear no one knows, but they
certainly are not afraid to climb cliffs and
crags that would frighten the average
white man half to death to even con-
template.

That all their children are not killed off
every month by falling from the eleva-

tions is shown by the fact that we saw a few of them playing in a little "clearing" in the brush at the bottom of the cañon. But we did not see them very long, for as soon as they got sight of the leading member of our party they fled to the brush and caves, and a pointer dog could not have flushed one five minutes later.

I have already described some of their strange methods of hunting game. In fishing they build dams in the mountain streams and poison the fish that collect therein with a deadly plant the Mexicans call *palmilla*, securing everything, finger-lings and all. They never tattoo, paint, or wear masks as far as I could ascertain. They are a strange, wild set of savages in a strange, picturesque country, a country that will repay visiting in the future should the means of transportation—rail-

A CLIFF DWELLING.

ways or better stage facilities—ever be sufficiently improved.

After leaving the wonderful Valley of the Churches it requires a night's rest before one is ready to give much admiration or attention to the magnificent scenery on every hand. It seems as if you had had a surfeit of the beautiful. I obtained a number of interesting sketches and photographs of these homes in the clouds. The photographs were taken under great drawbacks, as the days were stormy and cloudy, and even the lowest of the cliff dwellings were difficult of approach.

Just as we were descending a high mountain into the beautiful valley of the Tatawichic, we passed by an enormous rock on the steep trail of the mountain side that must have been fully three hundred feet high and not over thirty feet in diameter, which did not vary a foot from its base to its top, where it was rounded off like a half globe. It was green in color, looked exactly like a pitahaya cactus turned into stone, and seemed wonderfully unstable as seen from the trail that wound around its base on the steep descent. The name of the station at this point was Pilarcitas (Little Pillars), from the many curious and fantastic rock formations which assumed the shape of pillars, either singly or in groups of two, three, or more. The previous night had been very cold in the mountains, and the constant showers only increased the chill; so we found the little station houses the most welcome places of refuge as night came on.

The last station on this trail is about

STONE PILLAR ABOUT THREE HUNDRED FEET HIGH,
RESEMBLING CACTUS.

four or five miles from Carichic, and is in the center of a productive and well-watered valley. The little cultivation done there by the Indians shows a wonderful fertility of soil; in truth there are but few of the staple products that could not be grown in that portion of the country in the greatest abundance. At this last station of the Batopilas Company they start their private stages directly for Chihuahua. We remained over for a day, awaiting the departure of the regular diligence from Carichic.

While here I talked with an intelligent American, who had lived for many years in this country, about the Tarahumaris. He told me he had that season attended one of their foot races, a favorite pastime of these people. At this particular contest one of the fleetest and most endur-

ing foot runners in all the great band of
the Tarahumaris (or tribe of "foot
runners," as we know they are called)
was a contestant. That summer he had
made one hundred Spanish miles—about
ninety of ours—in eleven hours and
twenty minutes, in a great foot contest
near the Bacochic River, resting but once
for half an hour in this terribly long race.
The man, Mr. Thomas Ewing by name,
told me that he attempted to run this
foot runner a *vuelta,* (which is six miles
straight away and return, or twelve miles
altogether), Ewing using a horse; and
although the white man tried this three
times with three different horses, the
Tarahumari cave dweller beat him each
time. These contests of the Tarahumaris
are almost always very long and exciting. They make their bets with stock

of some kind, sheep, cattle, or goats, and
large numbers of these change hands on
the outcome of the races. In a letter to
me regarding these races, Mr. Ewing
writes of one of the runners:

" I was with him "—the Indian—" when
he was running his fifth round. It was
about eight o'clock in the morning, and he
was running at about eight miles an hour.
At that time his competitor was about
six miles behind him. I rode beside him
for about four miles, when my horse had
enough of it. There were a hundred
Indians or more to see the race, and they
had stations about every two miles on the
trail, where they stopped the runners,
rubbed them down, and gave them *pinola*,
a parched corn, ground fine and mixed
with water. The runners stopped one
minute, or about that, at each station for

rest. The Indian who won this race, although tired, finished in good shape, and took in about fifty dollars in stock."

These contests in running are said to be one of the amusements of even the wildest of the Tarahumaris, although I doubt whether many white men have witnessed them. Even as early as the days when Grijalva, the discoverer of Mexico, and Cortes, its conquerer, landed on its shores where now is the important port of Vera Cruz, within twenty-four hours after their appearance an Aztec artist had made perfect representations of the fleet, the kind and amount of armament, and correct pictures of the artillery and horses (although he had never seen such things before), and had transmitted them nearly two hundred miles by carrier to the City of Mexico, placing them in the hands of the Aztec Emperor Montezuma. Cortes afterward found that the Aztec, Tlascalan, and other armies of that portion of the country always moved at a run when on the march, thus trebling and quadrupling the military marches of the present day. This was the first intimation to Europeans of the endurance and swift-footedness of the natives of the great Mexican plateau, and a similar characteristic was found to be almost universal among the Indians of the plateau. But it was afterward discovered that the people most prominent in this respect was one in the far north of New Spain, hidden away in the fastnesses of the Sierra Madres, whose very name, as given by other tribes, Tarahumari, meaning foot runners, indicated their special excellence.

**THE END.**

# Index

Hermosillo, Mex. – 81, 82

Johnson, Dr. W. Derby – 47, 48

Juarez, Mex. – 48, 52, 54

La Ascencion, Mex. – 24, 34, 35, 42-43, 74
"La Cumbra" – 203, 270
Laguna de Guzman – 14, 30, 77
Laguna de Patos – 14
Laguna de Santa Maria – 14
Laguna Las Palomas – 15

"La Infinitad" trail – 272-73
La Laja station – 360
"La Naranja" plantation – 270
La Sierra de los Ojitos – 235
Las Palomas, Mex. – 17, 23, 24, 34
Las Palomas Mountain range – 16, 18

Macdonald, Mr. ___ – 48, 52
Mayo Indians – 106, 129, 177, 184
Mayo River – 132; valley, 333-36
Mazatlan, Mex. – 336
Mendoza, Alberto – 195
Mexican Central Railway – 132, 176-77, 343
Mexican-United States boundary – 4, 7, 8, 9, 16

Mexican War – 4, 104, 105
Mimbres River – 16
Montezuma – 194, 199, 385
Montezuma's Face – 22
Mormons – 35-41; Mexican colonies of, 35, 40, 47, 48, 50, 51, 52
Muller, Don Enrique – 153
Muñoz, Colonel ___ – 119

Naqueachic village – 223, 225
New Mexico – 10, 11, 16, 128; cliff dwellers of, 189, 190

Nogales, Mex. – 81, 117

Pacheco Peak – 27
Panascos River – 230
Parral, Mex. – 272
Pasigochic River valley – 213, 217
Pastrana silver mine – 322
Picacho de Torreon – 53
Piedras Verdes River – 47, 49, 50; valley, 48, 51, 55

Pilarcitas station – 378
Porfirio Díaz tunnel – 326
Porter, H. H. – 318
Potrero station – 345, 346, 348, 352
Prehistoric ruins – 48-69 passim, 190
Pueblo Indians – 191

Rio Grande (river) – 4, valley, 32

Rosario silver mine – 288

San Antonio silver mine – 322, 323
San Mateo Mountains, N.M., cliff dwellers of – 189
San Miguel and San Antonio hacienda – 313
San Miguel River – 49
Santa Eulalia mine – 327
Santa Fe Railway. *See* Atchison, Topeka and Santa Fe Railroad

Santa Maria River valley – 40
Santo Domingo Silver Mining Company – 324
San Vincente Island – 94, 97

Shepherd, Ex-Governor Alexander – 313, 339-40
Silver mimes of the Sierra Madre Mountain range – 45-47, 67, 68, 179, 195, 220, 268, 287, 288, 292, 293, 294, 307, 314-33
Sinaloa, Mex. (state) – 91, 128, 177, 219, 315, 333
Sisoguichic village – 226
Sonora, Mex. (state) – 10, 74, 112, 120, 128, 177, 219, 315, 333
Sonora Railway – 80-84, 107 109, 110, 113, 132
Southern Pacific Railway – 4, 10

Tanner, Captain U.S.N. – 91
Tapasita River valley – 52, 53, 56
Tarahumare Indians – 170-71, 180-247 *passim*, 343-77 *passim;* cliff dwellers, 186-88, 230, 233, 243, 244, 252, 260; as couriers, 202-05, 248, 381-85
Tatawichic River valley – 377
Teboreachic station – 357, 359

Tepehuane Indians – 184
Tlascalan Indians – 385
Todos Santos Mining Company – 324
Toltec Indians – 57, 61; ruins, 190, 355. *See also* Prehistoric ruins
Topolobampo, Mex. – 336
Torres station – 108, 110, 117

Tres Hermanas Mountain range – 18

Urique Barranca – 220, 251-64, 268-79, 357
Urique, Mex. – 266, 268, 280 283, 315, 319
Urique mining district – 266-98

Urique River – 255, 256, 283, 294, 300
U.S.S. *Albatross* – 91
U.S.S. *Congress* – 104, 105
U.S.S. *Portsmouth* – 104

Valley of the Churches.
See Arroyo de las Iglesias

Victorio, Chief — 17

Yaqui Indians — 106, 132,
177, 184; as guides, 109,
118, 119, 120, 121, 123,
125-26; as hostiles, 107, 129

Yaqui River — 132; valley,
333-36

Zacatecas mining district —
314